Corporate
Diversification

Corporate Diversification

Opportunities Created
by the Winds of Change

BROOKS FENNO

ARCHWAY
PUBLISHING

This book is a work of non-fiction. Unless otherwise noted, the author
and the publisher make no explicit guarantees as to the accuracy of
the information contained in this book and in some cases, names of
people and places have been altered to protect their privacy.

Archway Publishing books may be ordered through booksellers or by contacting:

Archway Publishing
1663 Liberty Drive
Bloomington, IN 47403
www.archwaypublishing.com
1 (888) 242-5904

Because of the dynamic nature of the Internet, any web addresses or links contained in
this book may have changed since publication and may no longer be valid. The views
expressed in this work are solely those of the author and do not necessarily reflect the
views of the publisher, and the publisher hereby disclaims any responsibility for them.

Any people depicted in stock imagery provided by Getty Images are
models, and such images are being used for illustrative purposes only.
Certain stock imagery © Getty Images.

ISBN: 978-1-4808-6306-4 (sc)
ISBN: 978-1-4808-6307-1 (hc)
ISBN: 978-1-4808-6308-8 (e)

Library of Congress Control Number: 2018905788

Print information available on the last page.

Archway Publishing rev. date: 7/5/2018

CONTENTS

PREFACE

This book represents my compendium of fifty years of work experience involved with, primarily, privately-owned businesses and enriched by personal marketing exposure in the fields of sales, advertising, and market research with firms of varying sizes and types. The text focuses on the *strategy of diversification.* For purposes of clarity, it contains examples of the many opportunities for diversification that the reader may encounter in today's corporate world.

Prior to founding my consulting practice, Salesmark (recently sold), I was active in corporate sales, sales management, product management, and national accounts management. At the conclusion of my direct corporate life, I created and developed my employer's European office equipment sales and service operation, headquartered in Germany.

During the forty subsequent years that I owned and operated Salesmark, I personally serviced 250 clients, extending from Germany to China. During that time frame, I taught marketing strategy in Babson College's MBA program, wrote a best-selling business book, *Helping Your Business Grow: 101 Dynamic Ideas In Marketing,* and served as a director of three companies, one public.

Before my corporate life began, I graduated from Harvard Business School. While a student at Harvard, I worked in market research at Gillette. Immediately after graduation, I joined Procter and Gamble in their brand management (advertising) program, followed by a corporate career in sales, product management, and overseas marketing management with Itek Corporation.

I am a veteran, having served as an officer in the 101st Airborne Division, and hold an AB degree from Princeton University.

INTRODUCTION

It is a rare business that can remain unchanged and continue to prosper. A successful business grows through the application of sound management- thinking and positive adaptation to the shifting environment of the marketplace in which it is situated. As an owner, CEO, or COO, you will benefit by thinking like a futurist. In so doing, you will be faced, at some point, with the option to pursue *diversification*. The concept of diversification offers three prime benefits: increased revenues, enhanced earnings, and, in most cases, corporate stability.

This book addresses the *why should*, the *what are,* and the *how to* of pursuing diverse growth opportunities through optimally intermixing an array of ingredients based, primarily, on the pursuit of *market segments* and *products or services*. The market segments section encompasses both existing and new market parameters. The products or services category includes the following: current products or services, modifications of these existing products or services, and the addition of new products or services.

This book's contents are directed to CEOs, business owners, and/or managers of both manufacturing and service companies[1] who market to other businesses (B2B), and, to a lesser extent, to owners who sell directly to the ultimate consumer (B2C). The text is punctuated with practical *TIPS* representing a compendium of concepts that may be encountered in transitioning a company successfully into its next level and stage of diversified growth.

---

[1] I have combined the service and product categories. I feel that a business service should be "productized" for optimal sales and marketing success, a concept inherent in both categories.

This book is *not* designed to address personal wealth diversification by individuals seeking to reduce their portfolio risk by acquiring partial ownership in a private company or by investing in multiple stock holdings. Nor is it designed for mid- to large-sized public corporations whose major diversification concerns include satisfying stockholder desires through positive quarterly earnings reports. Their interests are widely varied and include tax and other financial considerations beyond the scope of this book.

Should you, the reader, consider some aspect of diversification? *Yes.* Should you actively pursue growth through diversification? If so, what level of diversification should you seek, on a spectrum from a tweak to "trans-creating" your business into an entity with, basically, a new mission? That largely depends on your situation and your appetite for growth with risk.

This book does not attempt to answer these questions. Rather, it outlines the varied diversification options available and discusses certain of the risks involved.

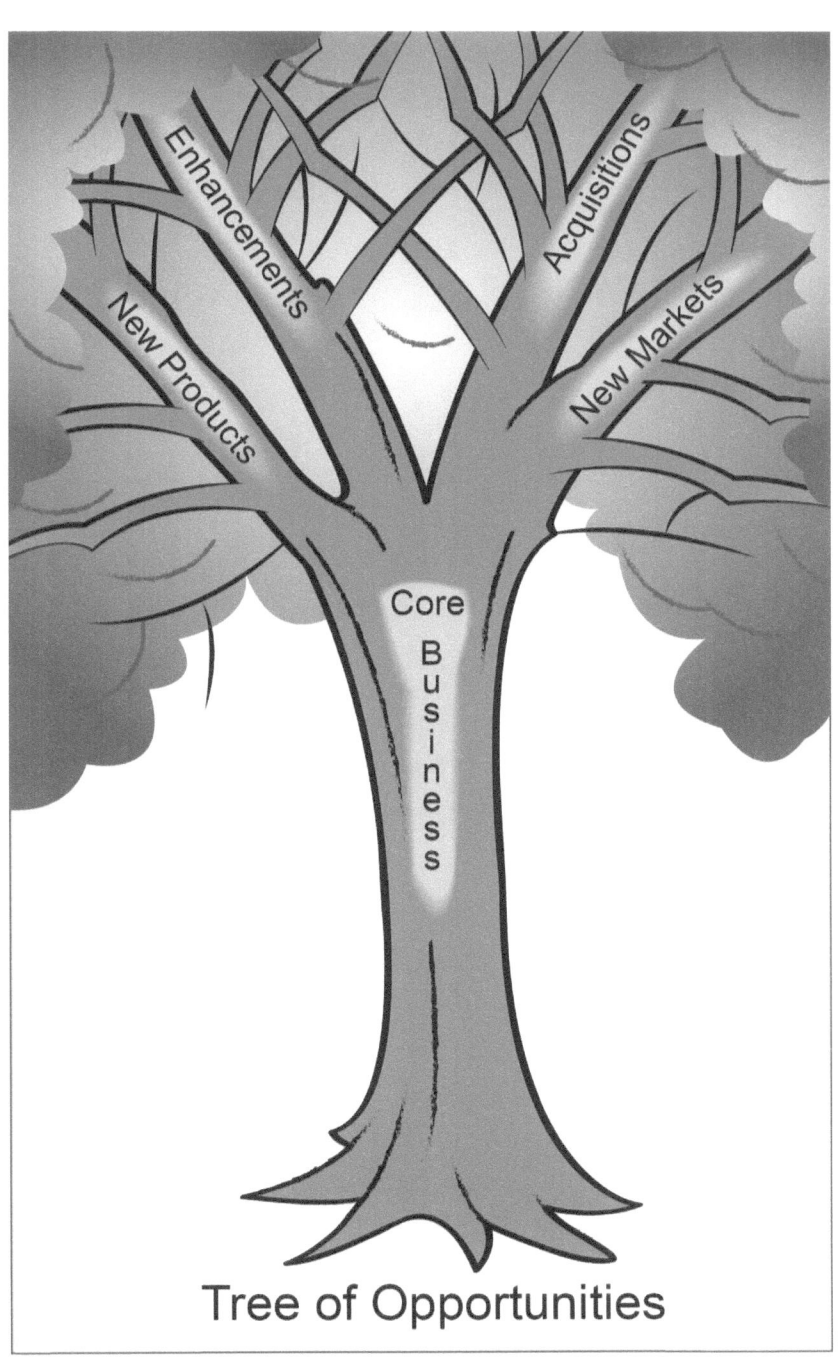

Tree of Opportunities

CHAPTER 1

Corporate Growth

The Table Setting

So you want to grow your business? Exercising prudent judgment regarding market shifts and opportunities may be sufficient for initial growth and short-term success. Or you may be in a niche market, protected from outside influences (for example, upscale, specialty publications like *Architectural Digest* or *Garden and Gun).* Finally, your core sales currently may continue to evolve on their upward spiral. However, these growth scenarios are unlikely to last forever.

> Tip: As the saying goes, "Before the river starts running dry, look for water elsewhere."

Assuming your goal is long-term growth—and if you have the drive, financial resources, and will to accept the time and risks involved—then *diversification* can become a bed-fellow.

There are many avenues available for diversification. They include facilities, personnel, equipment, processes, and particularly, markets. This book focuses on, but is not limited to, three forms of diversification: market development, product development, and pure diversification. The subject of this book is the configurations these forms of diversification, separately and in combination, might take.

So where do you stand regarding the strategy of diversification?

- Being reactive. Perhaps you are mildly curious—open to possibilities should such an opportunity cross your business threshold.
- Being a "forward thinker." Or you may recognize the need to expand into new areas if you are to continue to build revenues.
- Being pro-active. On a more aggressive note, you may currently be seeking ways of growing in a new direction.

Whatever your thoughts might be, this book illustrates the myriad of options you should consider and, possibly, elect to pursue.

The precursor to success in diversification, as is true in most any significant venture of substance, is *preparation*. Take football, for example. Bill Belichick, coach of the New England Patriots (and one of the most successful coaches of all times), is a meticulous preparer. He plans not only for this season (and next), but also plans, very thoroughly, for each-and-every game. The better your preparation, the more likely you are to optimize your success. Chapter 3, "Foundation: Modernize," addresses the preparation issue.

Let's return to the issue of growth. Why grow? Why not just continue as is? After all, you may control or possess an established company generating a sustainable income. Cutting to the chase, I identify but three basic scenarios facing you and your business: growth, decline, and status quo. In actuality, *status quo* can only be captured for but an instant—like a photograph. Thus, ultimately, you either grow or decline.

This growth-or-decline position holds true not only for our businesses but for each of us as individuals. We have our individual life cycle curves. On the personal side, ageing is a factor that we inevitably face. How do your energy level and health stack up? On the corporate side, we are strongly influenced by the marketplace in which our business functions. This marketplace is constantly evolving—shifting with the sands and winds of time. In what way is your marketing maturing?

The Tides of Change

I now spend my summers on the coast of northern Maine, with a short winter week on Florida's east coast. Being fascinated by the movement of the ocean, I observe the various tide changes, twice each day. In northern Maine, the tide fluctuates by some eighteen feet from ebb to high.

The impact of change is best illustrated by this perpetual shift in tides: change is ongoing, but it is not always visible to the naked eye. Unlike the ocean, however, the change we are experiencing, in business or personally, is one of evolution, not repetition; it is in constant motion in a multitude of directions.

As the noted columnist and author, Thomas Friedman, states in his most recent best-selling book, *Thank You For Being Late,* the three largest forces on the planet—technology, globalization, and climate change—are currently all accelerating at once. This creates an unprecedented rate of change for us all, in our business and personal lives. We find it hard to keep up!

Here are seven categories of change that affect each and every one of us on an evolving basis—some slowly, some on a daily basis:

- Population movement. Note emigration from strife-torn Near Eastern countries. We can readily observe the growth of other races in our local population mix—more noticeable, perhaps, in the eastern, southern, and western coastal regions of this country.

- National boundaries. A recent example is Britain opting to leave the confines of the European Union (Brexit).
- Buying trends. The switch to the Internet and e-commerce is having a profound impact on our lives in a multitude of ways.
- Market evolution. Changes are constantly occurring in *your* industry. Are you aware of them?
- Product innovation. Is a blockbuster product under development, or has it recently been introduced by you or competition?
- Family dynamics. We are all subject to them as we age. What are yours?
- Personal interests. We, too, change—besides ageing, our interests, energy level, and habits shift, as do those of our family.

The volatility of the marketplace is most prevalent and observable in the consumer field, but it also impacts the industrial market. Look at the energy industry. With the development of shale drilling for oil, it appeared that the United States would be exporting (rather than importing) oil in large quantities. But other countries latched onto this technology, and Near Eastern countries expanded their supply. Soon, we had an oil glut, which is noticeable today. Its impact has been felt in many industries, from oil producers to rail transportation to energy consumption practices.

Emerging in the field of energy are the natural forces of sun and wind. As collection sources become less expensive and as storage devices (i.e. batteries) become more efficient, we can expect soon to see a lessening of our dependence on fossil fuels like oil.

As Mike Nolan, vice chair of innovation and enterprise solutions at KPMG, LLP, recently was quoted as saying in *The Wall Street Journal*, "The pace of change today can be blinding. Business model transformations that once took ten to twenty years are now happening in as few as two to five. To stay competitive, leaders of innovative companies must be prepared to act before they are beaten to the punch by smaller, nimbler, and sometimes invisible rivals."

Change and Its Bedfellows: Opportunity and Risk

As the illustration below depicts, change creates opportunities, which are tied in and balanced with risk.

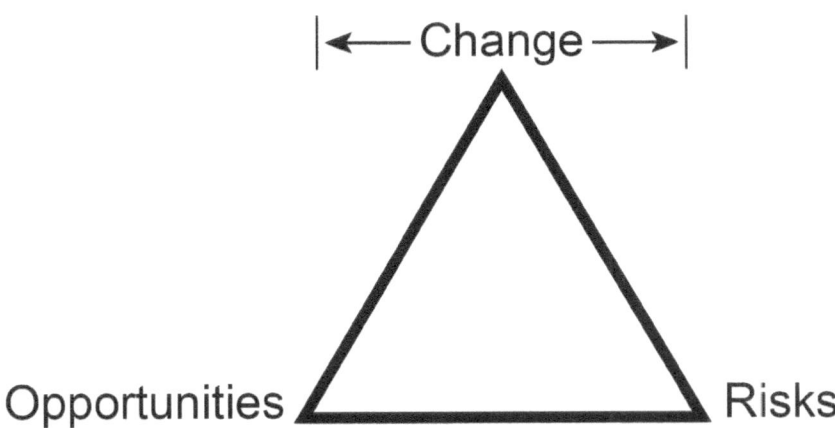

The opportunities afforded by diversification and the associated risks provide the grist of this book. Read on.

The accepted standard for measuring personal growth is *age*.

As we get older, we are less enthusiastic about having birthdays, but inevitably, they continue to happen. Corporate market-age is less well defined. We find it much harder to observe and measure. Many great business geniuses have failed in this respect—Ed Land of Polaroid being one. Arguably, he was the father of instant photography, but he failed to comprehend the implications of what he introduced. He did not envision the ramifications of what he had unleashed.

An analogy that I used in my business teaching is the *cloud of opportunity* concept. This cloud, representing buyer desires and needs, moves continually across our visual sky. Established businesses, like volcanic mountains, thrust primarily upward, ossify in size and structure, and thus lose the flexibility to track the horizontal movement of this cloud. This vertical rigidity often becomes their "death knell." However, it does provide an opportunity for new businesses (yours, for example?) to sprout, properly aligned with the latest center-position of the market cloud.

The rate at which the cloud moves across the sky appears to depend, primarily, on two factors: the nature of its market environment and consumer need/demand. Of course, increasingly, technological innovation is becoming a factor.

The Moving Cloud of Opportunity

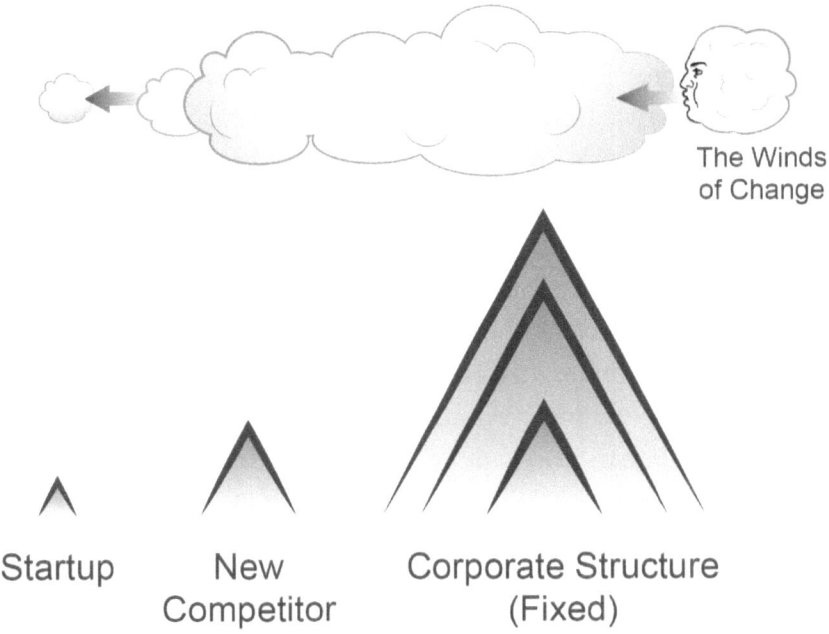

The Winds
of Change

Startup   New   Corporate Structure
           Competitor   (Fixed)

Take the previous example, Edwin Land of Polaroid or, another, Ken Olsen of Digital Equipment Corporation. Ken confidently predicted that the portable computer would never be a success. Thus, he did not pursue its development. How wrong this great man was!

A more recent example is my former employer, Gillette. For many years, it has enjoyed a virtual monopoly (70 percent US market share) in the razor-cartridge business. Gillette was acquired by Procter and Gamble, who, perhaps, envisioned extra sales by providing additional retail shelf space, excellent blade gross profit (Gillette reported a margin as high as 60 percent), and marketing muscle; but Gillette still represented a tempting longstanding, rigid, stationery target for outside competitive innovation. Gillette, governed by its stodgy parent Procter and Gamble, initially responded with what has been described as a "dismissive institutional smirk" to the inroads of competition.

Then along came Dollar Shave Club, followed by Harry's Razor Company. Both entered this three-billion-dollar market via the Internet sales route They took advantage of the shift in consumer purchasing habits from retail to less expensive online sourcing.

Today, Gillette's market share has dropped from 70 percent in 2010 to just above 50 percent as its parent company searches for ways to compete with these upstarts. Recently, Gillette has announced a product overhaul that will include a Fusion blade line with new technology at no added cost, plus lower-end competitive price options (see Gillette's new On Demand marketing program).

Examples of innovation-upstarts constantly appear even in growing markets like indoor lighting, where energy-efficient semi-conductor LED bulbs are replacing longstanding metal-filament bulbs. Light Bulb Company, a Boston startup, has recently introduced a new generation lightbulb that emits a warmer, more yellow-toned light than the LED counterpart. Ace Hardware and Staples now carry this new bulb. The originator of the electric light, General Electric (Thomas Edison), has recently announced that they are withdrawing from the home lighting field.

The marketplace for your business is evolving. Just how is it changing? At what rate? How are you likely to be thus impacted (within the next three to five years)? We naturally resist change. Just look at the shift in retail buying habits. A few years back, "box store" business was booming. These major brick-and-mortar department stores and mall merchandizers have been slow to embrace the customer switch to online purchasing. The e-commerce customer benefits from simplicity of shopping and typically lower cost. Contributing to the retailers' "foot dragging" is the reduced margin they receive. The latest figures indicate that e-commerce sales have edged ahead of local retail offerings. More on this important shift later in this book.

> Tip: It is important that you try to separate reality of this evolutionary change from your innate desire for stability.

One forthcoming evolutionary step, following on the heels of the Internet, is likely to be the field of artificial intelligence (AI). Take, for illustrative purposes, the Tesla automobile. Tesla driving accidents occur as unplanned environmental incidents take place. The software for the Tesla is then programmed to address these specific problem issues. Gradually, these few accidental incidents become still fewer, and so forth. The automotive initiative was launched by Tesla, whose "cloud of opportunity" is already being mimicked by NuTonomy, an MIT spinoff, plus close to a dozen similar startups funded by investors ranging from major corporations to small investors.

Another evolutionary field is medicine. For example, look at cancer treatments to note the progress in treating this illness. There are other new frontiers that you may have identified as more relevant to your personal and business interests.

An interesting exercise is to evaluate your (business and personal) receptivity to change. Where do you visualize this evolving change, in your case, on the scale between these two poles?

- *Slowly* disruptive. Change happens in all fields—eventually.
- *Rapidly* disruptive. Note recent market evolution in fields of communications, bio-science, technology, and transportation.

The speed and impact of this change is a critical issue for you to contemplate for both *defensive* and *opportunistic* reasons. They represent the two sides of the same evolutionary coin.

The Wave's Crest

Back to the symbolism of the ocean. Consider the position of the surfer. He or she seeks to ride the crest of a wave and not be over-run by its mass. Similarly, you want to be out front of the competition. It certainly helps if you get a head start on competition and then maintain that lead throughout the race.

> Tip: The best time to initiate evolutionary change is when a business is doing well, not when change is necessary.

Jack Welsh of General Electric always sought to maintain a position as number one or number two in a given market. He was willing to back away from a product when an elevated position was no longer sustainable and commit GE's resources elsewhere. Where do you fit? How are your offerings positioned over time? His successor, Jeff Immelt, has recently relocated GE to the Boston area. A prime reason for so doing was to position GE in a more favorable innovative environment than his Connecticut location. He is shifting GE from its core background, a machinery manufacturer, to a technology-driven company. This represents a diversified shift in strategic focus.

Growth Factors to Consider

Should you continue to expand your business in line with your current model or embellish it with diversification enhancements? One accepted and practical method of gauging the timing of that decision is to observe when your rate of revenue growth starts to level off or decline. Another indicator is when your sales team finds increased difficulty in identifying *new* viable buying prospects for your major offerings. A third is that you note competitors are becoming more numerous or effective in invading your prime market. The more successful you are (and have become), the more likely you are to attract competitors. *Actually, most any time is a good time to consider growth through diversification.*

The above factors may also be an indication that your market segment is maturing, thus no longer offering the evolutionary expansion opportunities formerly available. An easily identifiable analogy would be the restaurants in your urban area. A few restaurants likely have been in existence for years; some remain for several years—then are sold and emerge within a different décor and menu. Longstanding restaurants survive by offering basic fare, excellent service, and competitive pricing—and by *diversifying* (tailoring) their menu to accommodate the shifts in customer tastes. The fluid restaurant field thus illustrates both sustainability and change.

Resistance to Change

My training in practical psychology tells me that there are but *two* primary reasons to vary our habits and try something new. Virtually all significant personal change, outside of simple curiosity, is derived from one of these two reasons:

- An attractive opportunity—demonstrably better than what we are now experiencing.
- An undesirable current situation—an uncomfortable status quo.

Reflect on these two factors. In that we are creatures of comfortable habit, they are the underlying reasons why we change.

The Bottom Line

Essentially, most companies diversify to increase their revenue growth, albeit to enhance or preserve future earnings. Keep in mind this saying: *"Manage change—otherwise it manages you."*

Takeaways

In opening this book, this chapter addresses such issues as the shifting realities of change in its many forms as it will impact you and your business. It stresses the importance of recognizing and adapting to these market shifts and taking appropriate action on a timely basis. Be a leader, not a follower.

CHAPTER 2
Parameters of Diversification

The strategic pursuit of growth through diversification represents a significant step for any company. Diversification can be employed as an offensive or defensive strategy.

Diversification comes "clothed" in several forms and in a multitude of colors, styles, and sizes. Exactly what is *corporate diversification?* It is a somewhat amorphous concept, but it could be broadly categorized to include diverse activities. One example is the proposed link-up of Pfizer (the pharmaceutical giant) with Allergan PLC, effectively moving its legal headquarters to Ireland to reap the benefits of lower taxes. Another example, locally, is Boeing's construction of a new aircraft assembly plant in Charleston, South Carolina, which is non-union (versus their unionized plants elsewhere). The term *corporate diversification* can also be used in more limited configurations, as are highlighted in this book.

The contents of this publication focus on product and service forms of the dimension I classify as *horizontal* diversification. Vertical and other forms of diversification will be addressed, but with less emphasis, as they are more limited in application.

For purposes of clarification and discussion, I have arbitrarily created seven chapter-categories of diversification. Each category has its own element of *opportunity, cost,* and *risk.*

Category #1—*Enhancement* covers product or service changes that can be accomplished with minimal cost and effort within an existing company structure. This category includes *product line extensions.*

Category #2—*Current market/new product* addresses, essentially, new products or services that can be marketed to the current customer base.

Category #3—*Modified markets* covers pursuit of related markets in which the company's brand and reputation are of value, but product and sales support may differ from that now offered.

Category #4—*Current product/new market* relates to situations in which current products are sold into new market segments or new channels of distribution.

Category #5—*Vertical diversification* speaks to such systems as absorption of delivery service (i.e., adding it as an in-house service).

Category #6—*Mix and match* addresses common corporate practices in which a company pursues several product-market diversification programs simultaneously.

Category #7—*Reinvention* provides a rare look at companies that decide to enhance their strategic growth plan with a major product-shift into a divergent field.

As mentioned in the introduction to this book, the text covers *both* product and service offerings. This issue becomes further complicated in that the products category may be *subdivided* into both consumer and industrial segments. While these divisions differ in many respects, they have a common thread and are thus *combined,* as is clarified below.

A service offering can (and, from a sales standpoint, often should) be "productized"—a term briefly introduced earlier. By that I mean *packaging a service in a product's clothing for purposes of sales clarification.* In other words, describing a service as a product. For illustration, an automotive dealer may offer you a choice of three service packages (a common strategic sales gambit). Each package contains two or more bundled services offered at a single package price. It's simpler for both the dealer and customer to view the offering as a *packaged product.*

The method of sale differs significantly between the consumer and industrial markets, although the "productization" concept remains conceptually intact for both.

On the following pages, I start by defining marketing; then I offer my perspective; and finally, I illustrate the differences between marketing consumer and industrial products with a pie chart. The consumer product sales category depends heavily on advertising and promotion, while the industrial product is, typically, merchandized more through personal sales effort. The dividing line has to do with the per-item price of the product sold. A lower-cost item, whether product or service, cannot afford to carry the expense of a personalized sales approach.

However, when the consumer product is of sufficient size or value—say, as in an automobile—then both advertising and direct sales are employed.

The American Marketing Association defines marketing as "the activity, set of institutions, and process for creating, communicating, and delivering and exchanging offerings that have value for the customer, clients, partners, and society at large."

The AMA's definition is all-inclusive. My simplistic vision is that "marketing" consists of but three components: *market research* (an analysis of customer needs and buying habits), *advertising/ promotion,* and *sales.* These components all focus on the needs and wants of the buyer.

While the three components are represented in marketing both consumer and industrial products, the relative importance of the two categories differs notably, as is visually illustrated in the following pie chart. The percentage figures are examples and should not be construed as being otherwise.

Note the balance between segments as a shift occurs in the value of the individual item being sold.

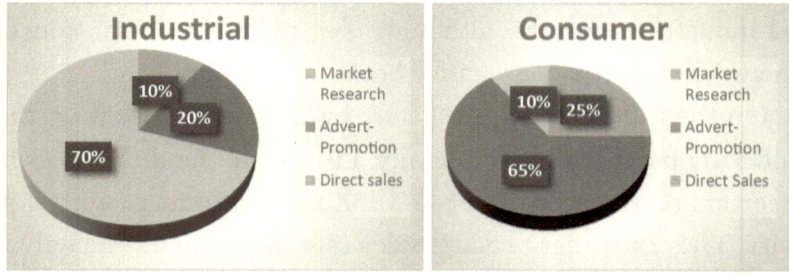

Risk-Reward Parameters

Until a company reaches and moves past its current-market phase of diversification, the *risk* factor is relatively minimal. For subsequent phases, the amount of risk should be carefully assessed. Risk works both ways. It is a two-edged sword. Change can be your ally, but it can work against you. If you don't take some risk, you will eventually be left behind.

One way to review risk is through the perspective of investment. The goal is to achieve a positive return on the growth potential of that investment.

> *Tip: The more complete the pre-program analysis is, the less the financial and operational risks become. Risk management is key.*

The chart below depicts the financial risks of the diversification options covered in the following five chapters.

	← Markets →	
	Current	New
P r o d u c t s	75%	25%
	50%	5-20%

These risk percentages are for illustrative purposes only. I have used these risk figures throughout my professional life, but I have, admittedly, not seen any numerical validation. Furthermore, keep in mind the competitive saying, "If the market pie isn't growing, the only way to increase your portion is to take someone else's slice."

So, that's the basic setting. But enough of the marketing preamble. Let's move into the option specifics in subsequent chapters.

Takeaways

This chapter sets the tone and outlines the approach and contents for our discussion on diversification. It defines "diversification" and its opportunities (and risks) for both consumer and industrial products and services.

In large measure, the reward-risk factor is related to the *synergistic gain* available through the diversification project. The greater the synergy achieved with your current product or service and the way it is marketed, the less risk you are likely to incur. Be careful not to overestimate the benefits or underestimate the cost of achieving this synergy. Remember, not all such opportunities are equal.

> *Tip: Your synergistic benefits should be identified and carefully assessed as part of the project or opportunity's vetting analysis.*

CHAPTER 3
Foundation: Modernize

A certain pre-existing state of corporate well-being is a requisite before taking any action to diversify in a way that will minimize risk. A sound corporate foundation, or platform, from which to expand is a vital base for launching a successful diversification program. Take the example the earlier illustration of a tree. When it is unable to support its fledgling branches in a heavy wind or snowstorm, it may topple. Furthermore, without a strong trunk, the tree will be unstable and is not likely to grow. I do not like to think of diversification as a panacea for lack of current marketing stability.

Along with a sound foundation, *preparation* is also critically important. Whether you are piloting a plane, scuba diving, or simply going on a challenging day's hike, preparation is vital to achieving success in addressing and overcoming potential mishaps along the way.

Besides structural considerations, an additional factor should be mentioned. Admittedly, there is nary a corporate executive who does not constantly face a myriad of ongoing problematic challenges in his or her average business day. However, these issues should generally be *under control* before pursuing diversification. How does a person judge attainment of such an operational level? My definition of control is a situation in which the company's ownership has stable coverage in the following three disciplines: (1) an up-to-date *internet program,* (2) a relatively stable *staff,* and (3) a *financial capability* sufficient to support both the current business needs and the risks involved in a diversification venture. Let's examine these three elements of control in turn.

A. *The Internet.* We have entered the electronic age. E-commerce has become a critical component in today's corporate culture. It is now a factor in almost everything we do. Take shopping, for instance. Formerly, we bought dry goods, staples, and building tools at our local retail store. The next evolution in our buying mode was to shop in the "big box" stores, with their attractive quantity pricing. Lately, the trend is to purchase online. E-commerce offers us still lower pricing and the convenience of shopping from, literally, home or office. According to a UPS survey, shoppers (consumers) made 51 percent of their purchases on the web in the first quarter of 2016. That figure is destined to continue to change upward.

An example of the fallout (ripple effect) is that mall owners have calculated that it is more advantageous to hand over property ownership to lenders (banks, etc.) than to attempt to restructure property debt as retail tenants move out due to their customers increasingly purchasing items online.

On the other side of this real estate shift, we have an increasing demand for urban industrial space to provide local warehouse storage for online call centers and retail delivery locations. This allows the Internet seller to accelerate response service to the customer. Ironically, the mall space formerly used by "big box" locations has been converted to these Internet-serving locations.

Large chains like Toys R Us (which recently filed for bankruptcy), Target, and Macy's are being hammered by the consumer trend to purchase via the Internet. Walmart now offers free shipping on many items to counter Amazon having no delivery charge.

This trend toward e-commerce is having a particularly strong impact on such staid consumer markets as newspapers and magazines. For example, *Self* magazine, a woman's publication, is converting entirely to digital in early 2017, excepting occasional feature-issues based on health and wellness topics.

There has been a trickle-down or ripple effect from the Internet concept to even the smallest of stores. For example, an owner of a boutique Connecticut clothing store confided to me that she now is forced to deal with "showrooming." This phrase describes the shopper who comes into her store, selects a fashionable dress, tries it on to establish a proper fit and look, takes it home to confirm details, and then orders it online at a lower price. This "customer" returns the original dress to the store the next day!

A growing company's website and supporting marketing program need to be updated before management actively undertakes any diversification program. A basic Internet package consists of two distinct parts: the corporate website and the promotion thereof. The common vernacular to describe the latter is SEO (search engine optimization).

- The website should be accessible, informative, and responsive.

     The *accessible* portion refers to how the website interacts with all prospect-accessible media (cellphones, mobile devices, apps, laptops, desktops, etc.).

     The *informative* category refers to it being properly coded (with SEO) for the provider's identification by search-programmatic media.

The *responsive* function refers to it being constructed to drive responders to informative corporate content on the website. This may include specific text from within the web catalog.

Achievement of the above represents a complex and demanding corporate responsibility best executed by a digital expert, not a friend or business companion. Design responsibilities include mastering social media (Twitter, Facebook, LinkedIn profiles, etc.), blogs, webinars, video, YouTube channels, virtual trade shows, etc.

> *Tip: Make certain you obtain feedback that permits continual editing and updating of media and message receptivity. This is a must-do!*

B. *Staff structure.* As in any undertaking, the preparation or planning phase is critically important. An individual (you or a subordinate) needs to spearhead any diversification project to have it properly launched.

> *Tip: Ultimately, someone must take personal ownership of the diversification program if it is to succeed.*

> *Tip: The competency of the selected individual will, likely, be reflected in the rate of return from the new venture.*

Caution: Beware of placing an individual in charge who has not heretofore exhibited leadership qualities and who does not have the respect of his or her peers. The selected individual will, ultimately, be required to sell the resulting change factors to the other members of the management team.

Keep in mind that the individual in charge must be able to integrate the selected diversification program into the corporate culture. Thus, he or she must be able to overcome normal resistance to change exhibited by fellow employees. The new program may require this individual to add new tasks to his or her current workload—an unwelcome outcome.

Larger companies have established sales departments and, likely, a marketing unit as well. If your firm is of such corporate size, is its marketing arm capable of creating, developing, and launching a successful diversification program?

Tip: Consider how you are going to compensate the lead individual(s) for taking on the extra diversification workload.

Other staff checklist considerations:

- Fellow staff members. They too must "buy in" to your diversification plans. Will they be the ones to develop the formal implementation plan?
- Sales personnel. How and who will assess the diversification option? Who is going to do the field-selling of the diversified product or program? How will it be launched? How will its success be measured (method and frequency)?
- Ancillary services. Do you have adequate accounting, human resources, and promotional support for a diversified growth program? What about shipping and storage and resources?

- Your involvement. Even if staff personnel are available, your time will be required as well.

C. *Financial capabilities.* Of course, financial demands will depend upon the nature of the diversification project. Monies will be required to investigate the diversification concept, to develop it, and then to launch it.

> *Tip: Be prepared to spend up to half again the amount initially budgeted for the completed diversification program before a positive financial return is realized. Watch the cash flow requirement.*

Funding sources exist both within and outside the company. Internally, several operational sources are available for smaller companies, such as the following:

- Available cash.
- Receivables. Can they be tightened through prompt-payment incentives?
- Payables. Can they be stretched to provide available working capital?
- Credit card debt. This is and has always been a funding resource for the small company. However, it is an expensive way to finance long-term.

From the outside:

- Bank loans. If you have a good relationship with your banker and bank, this is an excellent resource. As an option, ask about a Smaller Business Administration (SBA) loan.

- Friends and relations. This is an oft-used source for small companies, but one that can lead to personal issues down the line. Be careful, as it can puncture a friendship!

- Venture capital. This could come from a variety of sources, such as friends, business associates, and, more recently, publicly raised "cloud" funding. Cloud funding can be risky in that your idea may be "borrowed" by another company that claims invention priority. However, cloud funding is a viable method of generating start-up funds for, particularly, technical products and innovative services.

D. Circles of support. In preparing for any form of diversification, first discuss the concept with a select inner circle of trusted personnel, both inside your company and, as appropriate, outside. When an acceptable and realistic plan has been developed, then review it with a larger circle on a need-to-know basis.

> *Tip: Seek out problems you don't expect to exist. Eventually, somehow, many will surface.*

Takeaway

Make sure you are generally comfortable with operational conditions within your firm. Only when you feel secure with the above-described structure should you consider actively pursuing a program of diversification.

CHAPTER 4

Diversification: The Journey

A journey can consist of many stages, each with its twists and turns and each with unexpected challenges. This is also true of diversification.

I have always enjoyed mountain climbing. In my mid-life years, I tackled Mt. Kilimanjaro in Kenya. The initial phase of that climb required a day or two of gradual ascent leading up to the base of the mountain itself.

The initial step in any diversification program conveniently starts in your backyard. It involves taking full advantage of your current saleable assets (products or services) by modifying them to broaden their appeal to your current market. This approach may require some product alterations, but no major shifts otherwise. In fact, this "broadening" activity may serve to pep up your sales program by giving your sales staff additional talking points with customers and prospects.

I refer to this initial step as developing *supplemental products*. The most common forms of these supplemental products may be classified as *product enhancements* and *product line extensions*.

> Tip: Regardless of how these supplemental products are identical, they should be tracked individually, categorized by sales and profit contributions.

But when does the mountain (diversification) appear in full view? In the previous chapter, we explored the breadth of the diversification concept. For our purposes, Wikipedia's definition of diversification best serves our needs: "a corporate strategy in which a company acquires or establishes a business other than of its current product." This definition lacks the breadth and specificity required for this chapter. When *diversification* is mentioned, we think of a major change in a business's product. But the edge boundaries of diversification are a bit fuzzy.

Most marketers, when discussing diversification, think of it as a one- dimensional option—*horizontal*. While this book focuses on horizontal diversification, I would be remiss if I failed to mention the *vertical* element. Vertical diversification, noted earlier, can be both downward (i.e., *diversification through delivery*) and upward (i.e., *product remodeling*). In short, these vertical factors may significantly impact sales revenues; thus, they shouldn't be ignored.

Back to product line extensions. Within this category there exist a myriad of sub-categories ranging from tweaking products to more significant product alterations.

Let's start with a "product tweak" (commonly known as a product enhancement). I choose to mention this specific category as a diversification subject even though it may not fit in with Wikipedia's definition. My rationale is that a marketing tweak represents the very first, low-risk step in launching a *"growth through diversification"* program.

Let's take some examples of tweaks. If you simply reposition a product in your advertising campaign, is that a form of diversification? Or if you reprice a product, does that constitute a form of diversification? Or supposing you alter a product's packaging design, and thus its image; could that be considered diversification? As you can readily see, there is a fine line in determining precisely what constitutes true *diversification* versus *product enhancement* or *product line extensions*. Keep this subtlety in mind as you read further.

A simple tweak was recently brought to my attention at a company's annual meeting. It seems that they requested and received an industry-recognized quality performance rating, like the Federal Government's Occupational Safety and Health's (OSHA) approval, that enabled them to expand their customer base.

A more involved example of a product line extension was McDonald's introduction of their all-day breakfast in early 2015. Their new CEO, Steve Easterbrook, expanded their breakfast menu offering past their scheduled 10:30 a.m. breakfast cutoff. The broader availability of breakfast items (available throughout the day) increased both the total per-customer expenditure at lunch hour *and* the number of luncheon customers. Presumably, this line addition has more than offset the likely higher margins formerly generated by the lunch menu items that have been replaced by breakfast fare.

Starbucks Corporation is moving more dramatically afield by diversifying beyond its coffee roots to meet continued growth goals inherent in its five-year strategic plan. It has extended its *horizontal* diversification offerings by adding drinkware, collectibles, and a telephone app. It is also licensing, worldwide, a LEED-certified line of "green" retail buildings that are energy efficient and environmentally desirable. Now, that is extreme diversification!

Starbucks is also diversifying *vertically* by expanding into the high-end coffee shop market. Howard Schultz is stepping down as Starbuck's CEO and pioneering an effort to refresh Starbuck's brand by revolutionizing the way Americans view and consume coffee. These "shops" will sell coffee at prices up to twelve dollars a cup!

The retail banking industry calls this "cross-selling." If a customer has a checking account, why not sell him/her a credit card, a mortgage, or wealth management service? On the surface, this strategy seems quite simple and desirable. However, in spite of strong management quota-backing (see 2016 Wells Fargo's issues), this approach to diversification (current market/new products) has been largely resisted by banking customers. Initially, it appears that these customers have already adopted other sources of supply.

> Tip: Before adding ancillary products, you should assess the prospects' attachment to their current providers.

A recent "growth enhancement" example of diversification is provided by Elon Musk, Tesla (Motors') CEO. With virtually unanimous shareholder approval, Tesla, the electric car producer, has acquired SolarCity Corporation, the largest solar panel installer in this country. You may ask, what is the synergy element in this acquisition?

Elon's plan is to create an integrated clean-energy company—a one-stop shop for solar panels, batteries, and electric cars. A solar-paneled home roof will, reportedly, look better, last twice as long, and cost less (half the normal tiled-shingle price). Foremost, it will generate much of the energy needed to power both the owner's home and the household's all-electric car. Other references to Elon and his varied accomplishments are noted in the Appendix.

A different kind of "tweaking" is illustrated by the Maine Seacoast Mission (MSM), a 110-year-old non-profit organization. They were founded to provide health and support services to some two hundred island inhabitants via MSM's traveling vessel, the *Sunbeam*. The number of islands thus served has dropped as island residents relocated to the mainland over time, reflecting the decline in the fishing industry and their desire for a more balanced lifestyle. Today, MSM offers advanced medical diagnostic and educational services to a rural Maine population, regardless of location.

In accordance with a newly developed funding solicitation strategy, MSM now targets five vertical customer segments (offering the same product to a redefined customer base). These segments are (1) individual (state and local) agencies, (2) past donors, (3) wealthy prospects, (4) foundations, and (5) churches. Each of these will be approached with a different benefit package tailored to their specific interests. The basic product offerings haven't changed; only their promotion package has. Diversification?

Should you or your company wish to proceed with any diversification strategies, your company should undertake the product or service tweaking, or product-line modification, that might be appropriate for your situation. This initial approach minimizes expense, effort, and risk.

When we reflect on the concept of product diversification, we might want to, initially, consider a higher- or lower-priced product line. Restaurant menus illustrate an aspect of this. They offer "chef specials" that are frequently repeated if successful and eliminated if not. This editing tactic can serve as a flexible model for *service* providers. However *pure* diversification is more difficult for *manufacturers* to institute, as an increase in cost of goods sold (CGS) and inventory investment is required.

Another parameter, known to all, is the fast-growing distribution channel represented by *the Internet* (mentioned in the last chapter). It's more than a tweak, but should it be classified as pure diversification?

The *no* answer is that it represents corporate evolution in our technically sophisticated society. It can involve, in its distribution garb, simply contacting the current customer/prospect base through a different medium. The *yes* answer is that online shopping may reach new customers, those to whom brick-and-mortar shopping did not appeal. We illustrate this with the example of one company, MicroMedia, in the next chapter.

Furthermore, this e-commerce channel should be viewed as more than a sales tool. The fallout from this approach represents an entirely different method of distribution and thus impacts profitability. In this respect, it is a form of vertical diversification.

The previous chapter discussed the Internet and referenced the web page as a response vehicle which can serve as an upscale "brochure" to describe a firm's offerings. It may also be classified as a sales tool—one that reaches out to prospects *new* and *old*. Thus, it becomes a modern form of promotion replacing (or supplementing) direct mail and space advertising (trade journals for the industrial market, TV/radio broadcasting and magazines for consumers). A firm's web page fills that requirement.

Look for further comments on Internet marketing in chapter 10, "Implementation."

As you can thus appreciate, a fine dividing line exists between product line enhancement and diversification. I classify the American Automobile Association's offerings of products and services as evolving into the classic realm of multi-faceted diversification.

I was introduced to AAA many years ago as the organization that I, as a young driver, should call when my car broke down or needed a battery recharged. My sister was told they would change her tire if requested (my father had taught me how to change tires).

But now, with its sizeable membership, AAA has widely

expanded their offerings to include ancillary products in the automotive market. They have diversified by broadening their product line to cover insurance, car rentals, travel agency services (a full-service travel company), safeguarding credit, protection against identity fraud, and even help in buying and paying for your new car—impressive, to say the least!

This introduces the interesting issue of timing—i.e., *when* should a business owner consider product enhancement? Competition, corporate growth and success, opportunity, and a myriad of factors typically are involved in deciding *whether* to enhance, *when* to enhance, and *which* product enhancement options to pursue.

The most common form of product enhancement is introducing a *like* model, more-or-less expensive than the corporation's prime offering. A "model offshoot" is usually simple to design but tricky to integrate into the product mix without jeopardizing sales and profitability of the basic product.

A straightforward example is provided by my former client, Zipwall LLC. Its founder, Jeff Whittemore, realized, through his prior employment in the flooring industry, that there was a need for a dust barrier mechanism to help contractors contain (and thus control) dust emissions during commercial and residential construction and remodeling.

In 1997, Jeff launched ZipWall with a product called the KT12— an aluminum extension pole (five to twelve feet, adjustable) with a special spring-loaded top. This enabled the user (contractor) to secure the pole effortlessly to both floor and ceiling. A pole package sold for $139. Initially, it was marketed directly through remodeling magazines.

The KT12 was an immediate hit. It provided contractors with a simple vehicle for suspending separately purchased plastic dust-barrier sheets during the construction process. Early on, he *extended* his line with a twenty-foot pole for commercial contractors who worked in buildings with high ceilings. He priced this new package 30 percent above the KT 12. This was his initial product-line enhancement.

As frequently happens with a successful product, competitors start appearing with, often, inferior products at a reduced price. Jeff held them off with patent infringement lawsuits, but he realized ZipWall might benefit from introducing its own lower-priced line.

His second product-line enhancement came in 2010 with the introduction of the ten-foot ZipPole, priced 30 percent below the KT12 line. The smaller pole was made of less expensive steel. It was successfully integrated into ZipWall's marketing mix with minimal "cannibalization" of the KT12 line's sales.

> *Tip: Try to maintain the same absolute-dollar cost of goods sold as with the lower-priced product to minimize the potential financial impact of having the consumer shift to the purchase of a less-expensive model.*

> *Tip: Treat the "modified product line" separately from the major product or service offering. It should have a separate marketing plan and its own financial tracking category.*

A more recent odd-ball example of the emergence of a lower-priced product line introduction is that of Mylan NV and its generic EpiPen. Mylan elevated the price of its newly acquired lifesaving drug-dispensing EpiPen to six hundred dollars per pen.

Public outcry was such that Mylan then offered two generic pens for a combination package-price of three hundred dollars.

Another such recent example is the action of Mondelez International. Mondelez announced that it is changing the shape of its popular chocolate bar Toblerone. This redesign includes offering fewer ridges of chocolate per bar—an effective way of reducing product (ingredient) costs of chocolate from 170 grams to 150 grams per bar and thus offsetting the increasing ingredient and manufacturing costs.

Of course, the per-bar price remains the same. Candy bar producers frequently adopt this practice, but their brand (and price) must be well-established. Otherwise, they are vulnerable to a consumer sales decline.

Takeaways

These illustrations point out the extensive range of diversification possibilities available in a company's product offerings. These various tweaks, or product modifications, represent the first step in a diversification program. They can be implemented with minimal product-line alteration and no major market shift.

CHAPTER 5

Current Market—New Product

Once your company's product-enhancement options have been developed, a sequential advancement step is for you to introduce a new product into your current market. This *current market—new product* option offers a *multitude* of possibilities, each of which will be individually discussed. In short, they include the following:

- Technical upgrades
- Inventions
- Distributed products
- Pure new products or services

Idea Identification

Before we consider possible new product or service diversification concepts, let's consider how and where we might look for viable concepts. Basically, there are two places to search: within the company and outside your firm.

- *Inside. You* represent a critical "thought-point." Undoubtedly, you already have some product ideas sitting in your mental warehouse. Start by identifying them. The next best idea-source is *your employees.* Begin with your senior staff.

Tip: Challenge (and motivate) employees to develop new product ideas.

Include the sales team. Don't ignore the hourly employees. A contest can be helpful in stimulating their thoughts.

Tip: By including all employees in the search process, you will stimulate an employee awareness mentality and thus motivate overall creativivity.

- *Outside.* Many external sources exist within your market. Begin with your *key customers.* Other sources include *knowledgeable individuals* who are familiar with your brand and reputation. One of your most productive sources is likely to be your *suppliers.* They know you and the marketplace you serve. They also may know what products your competitors are developing. *Independent sales representatives* are a particularly viable source for suggestions.

Tip: If you don't seek out and ask others, you may overlook valuable suggestions.

Speaking of asking, don't forget *trade association personnel.* I have one client, Bixby International, whose personnel visit trade shows primarily to seek out new ideas by contacting competitors, buyers, vendors, and other show participants. *Editors of trade publications* are another viable source in this regard. You might even want to contact professors or researchers who are or have been involved in the forefront of your field's development.

On the surface, the current market/new product category may appear to need little conceptual clarification. But what about a modified product and/or an expanded market? Technology upgrades provide a perfect example. A newly engineered, high-tech system or device logically represents a notable improvement over an existing product. Furthermore, a high-tech product could offer features (performance and price) that allow it to penetrate a broader market than it currently serves.

Take, for example, MicroMedia of New England, Inc. Arthur "Sandy" McGinnes, the founder and owner, was faced with declining sales for his core business: microfilm and microfiche services. His products focused on photographically indexing records for commercial customers. Looking into the future, he could visualize the impact of electronic imaging.

He pieced together a system called CAR (computer assisted retrieval), which enabled him to offset his declining sales. Four years later, that process became outmoded. He then transitioned into electronic scanning. In ten years, MicroMedia grew from $1 million to $10 million in sales, with a $4 million EBITA (Earnings Before Income & Taxes) when he sold out in 2001. Today, the enterprise that, in turn, acquired his acquirer, boasts profitable sales of over $1 billion with twenty-four thousand employees.

There were two keys to Sandy's success. He personally took charge of searching out new opportunities in these ways:

1. Asking key customers what advanced supply-source technology they were evaluating.
2. Determining what the leaders in his industry were recommending.

Sandy's core knowledge certainly was enhanced by joining his industry's trade group (he eventually became its president). Once he perceived the direction in which the document industry was evolving, he acted by identifying and pursuing small, emerging, and growing firms with whom he might partner.

On a closing note Sandy eagerly offered the following additional advice:

> Tip: Every potential sale is an opportunity to visualize growth in a new direction.

In other words, he always remained alert to the potential possibilities of the applications that his product sales had unearthed.

> Tip: Change is occurring particularly rapidly in today's high-tech world. This creates an entry opportunity, but also the risk of equally rapid obsolescence.

Let's look at a few unusual examples of new products being introduced into existing markets. These may further stimulate your thoughts.

Partners Health Care, a leading New England health care provider that serves many local hospital chains, including Brigham and Women's Hospital and Massachusetts General Hospital, has developed a sophisticated software package. One of its member organizations, Dana Farber Hospital, has packaged this software *under its own label* and is marketing it to its smaller hospital subsidiaries. This illustrates how an organization can take someone else's product, refine it, and market it to its own customer base—a distribution form of sales diversification.

Another unusual example occurred at the *Boston Globe*. Its new owner, John Henry, a financial investor who also owns part interest in the Boston Red Sox, appears to have been attempting to drive down publication costs to fund his acquisition expense. He relocated the Globe's headquarters and lowered printing costs by reducing the size of the paper, farming out production, and lessening the quality of the newspaper stock. In an attempt to lower distribution costs he switched to a new hard-copy distributor, ACI Media Group, headquartered on the West Coast, to service his home-delivery subscriber base of over two hundred thousand in the New England market.

John might appear to have failed to realize the unexpected consequences of such a delivery changeover, and equally importantly, he didn't seem to fully understand that the early morning home-delivery service was, in fact, a tangible reason that subscribers purchased hard copies. Conceptually, he was diversifying by *replacing* an existing "product" (i.e., a distribution service) with a like product. For the next several weeks, there was delivery chaos. Subscribers were alienated as deliveries were made late or not at all. Poor planning! If he intended to reduce the number of hard copies sold (unlikely, but possibly in favor of online subscribers), he inadvertently succeeded!

In hindsight, the *Boston Globe's* management reportedly may have failed to conduct an effective due-diligence investigation for the changeover strategy. A major problem was engaging a contractor with no knowledge of or experience in the local geographic market area and who had a route delivery plan markedly different from that of his predecessor.

Takeaways

Pursuing the strategy of bringing a new product into your existing market is a very reasonable diversification option. However, it does require a significant investment in money and time and does involve a certain level of risk. This risk can and should be minimized with a proper due-diligence investigation.

As illustrated in this chapter, a very broad range of diversification options for your business most likely exists. *Every* aspect of your business should be reviewed in seeking such opportunities.

CHAPTER 6

Related Markets

A frequently pursued alternative step for expanding a company's revenue base is to transition into a related market or market segment. Sometimes this change is designed to enhance existing sales, and sometimes it is done out of necessity in cases where currently served markets no longer present opportune growth options—the cloud of opportunity's focal point may have shifted.

Related markets are a complex and difficult concept to define distinctly. They fit somewhere between tweaking (product line extension) and new market diversification. My definition is admittedly arbitrary, but I want to make certain all such related options are addressed.

To qualify as a "related market," in my opinion, a diversified product or service should include a minimum (besides the basic products or services) of many or most of the following six factors connected to the company's existing capabilities:

- Common location (office and shipping facility)
- Current, unified management staff
- Same distribution channel(s)
- Same dealer network
- Alignment with current rep force focus
- Overlapping customer base

Take Xerox Corporation as an illustration. It was experiencing shrinking sales of its copiers and printers. Xerox tried to diversify by acquiring a service-based company, Affiliated Computer Services Incorporated, which provides back-office services for companies and governments. By 2015, this changeover to document, bill processing and other like services generated over 50 percent of Xerox's top line according to the *Wall Street Journal* (November 24, 2015).

Unfortunately for Xerox, this shift did not result in increased profitability. It was not the growth panacea that Xerox's management had sought. It left Xerox vulnerable to outside investment intervention as corporate earnings continued to decline. Enter the noted activist Carl Icahn. At his urging, Xerox plans to split into two public companies: a $7 billion services provider (104,000 employees) and an $11 billion documents provider (40,000 employees). The grass may look greener on the other side of the street, but that form of thinking isn't always valid.

Staples is desperately searching for a new marketing approach. Just recently, Staples announced that it was shifting its advertising focus from its foundation of selling low-priced office supplies through its retail stores to the Internet. This new plan will feature Staples's own delivery system, which will offer product service and repair as well as shipping.

Nike Corporation is best known for its basketball sneakers. But Nike has broadened its offerings considerably. Besides sneakers, it markets sports shoes ranging from running shoes to soccer shoes with cleats. Furthermore, it now sells various lines of clothing, including Tech Fleece jackets (to colleges), plus football-branded and custom-logo shirts. This is an example of diversification through its current market channel in the form of a significant product line extension.

Amazon provides another example. Best known for its low

price and customer fulfillment capabilities, Amazon continues to add to its product offerings. In May 2016, Amazon announced that it would offer its own branded food line (private label store branding continues to increase market share versus nationally recognized brands). By subsequently acquiring Whole Foods Market it further enhanced its involvement in the retail food market. Through its Prime Now 2-hour delivery service Amazon has launched a new method of competing by offering the grocery shopper added purchasing convenience.

An excellent, recent example is Viking Cruises (a Swiss company). Its principle arm is Viking River Cruises, which operates some nine river-cruise vessels. Viking has introduced a sister division, Viking Ocean Cruises, which has launched a new ship, the *Viking Star*. This vessel differs markedly in size from its river brethren (930 passengers, up from 320) and is ocean-going; but from an accommodation and functional standpoint, it has many similarities to its river-cruising kin. It also focuses on excursions and culture. Its marketing target passenger-group is affluent retirees (kids under eighteen not welcome). There are no water slides or rock-climbing walls!

Viking's prime value to this form of diversification is the similarities within the target audience. Employing its same marketing formula, Viking is thus able to broaden the experiences of (and thus revenue from) its existing and, presumably, satisfied customer base to compete in the ocean-going vacation market.

Viking has just announced a World Cruise package (128 days- $50,000 minimum). Not only does this promotion enhance Viking's ocean-going cruise capabilities but it positions Viking as a world travel provider.

On a much smaller scale, TruckCourier has pursued what is

best described as an entry into a related market. TruckCourier is a regional (Northeast market area), point-to-point, large-product, heavy-shipment, same-day trucking company. It utilizes independent contractors with their vehicles to provide expedited pick-up and delivery service. Recently, its founder, Arthur Brussard, acquired a small-shipment Boston-area delivery service that utilizes smaller cargo vans to make its deliveries.

While TruckCourier's dispatch team, customer service personnel, and sales personnel could easily handle both types of orders (larger and smaller), both the customers and the independent contractors were initially confused as to who would be delivering which orders and at what rate. By necessity, this issue had to be resolved before the acquisition was effectively finalized.

Still within the transportation field, Uber, the emerging "taxi company" that we read about, is morphing into a global logistics service. Uber Cargo offers a van capability that will transport various-sized items. The client has the option of accompanying the shipment. Again, this illustrates the opportunities available through related market diversification.

Takeaways

This category illustrates the interrelationship between product line extensions and diversified offerings. Xerox's situation didn't produce the desired strategic synergy. The outcome from Nike and Uber has yet to be determined, but their financial commitment was, proportionally, far less than Xerox's. In these three cases, note an important principle:

> *Tip: The* <u>*risk*</u> *factor increases as the perceived distance from the prime offering increases.*

CHAPTER 7
New Markets

As the chart in chapter 2 illustrates, the difficulty of selling an existing product line into a new market segment is a challenging concept from the standpoint of managing risk. I have conducted numerous studies for manufacturers who sought to take advantage of this potential opportunity and, upon a due-diligence investigation, wisely decided *not* to proceed further.

The "opportunity" that many visualize by expanding the sales of their current product line into a new market is that they are already making a product and would like to benefit from simply increasing their production run. Thus, for them, no new product development effort is required. However, there are a variety of hurdles they face even if their product can be utilized in the proposed market.

Four problems stand out *even when the expanded product-line outperforms the existing competitor's existing products and may be less costly*—both big *ifs:*

- New buyers lack inertia to change purchasing habits.
- Both buyers and channel members lack familiarity (comfort) with the new product or service being offered.
- While competitive reaction is often slow to develop, it will eventually appear, with its intensity proportional to the damage inflicted (e.g., price matching).
- Sellers lack understanding (knowledge) of the operation of the new market itself.

Another way of viewing this issue is to remind the reader that customers change their buying/using habits for, predominantly two reasons: They are motivated to change by perceiving a significant advantage in pursuing the newly-afforded opportunity. Or they are significantly dissatisfied with their current situation (price, product quality or service).

Obviously, the greater a person's current investment (time and money) with a particular "modus operandi" the less that person will be inclined to make any change. In chapter 10, we will address techniques for overcoming these and similar hurdles.

Geographic Market Diversification

The most commonly pursued and perhaps the most fertile application for current product—new market diversification is one of geographic expansion. These geographical limits can extend from the next town (a local service) to the overseas market.

Just a passing mention on the next-town diversification option: the readership is undoubtedly familiar with the example of restaurants that have opened new facilities, under their existing name, in a neighboring town. The hope here is that their local brand recognition will carry into a like environment. In Boston, we have Aquitaine Restaurant, which has successfully established new facilities in both Chestnut Hill and Dedham, equally affluent suburbs some dozen miles to the west and southwest respectively. Diners in these neighboring towns are familiar with the Aquitaine name and offerings.

A farther-reaching geographic example is Fisher Engineering Company, a Maine-based manufacturer of truck-mounted snowplows for whom I consulted in the early 1980s. Dean Fisher, its owner, contacted me to determine whether he might be able to extend his market-reach into the Midwest. He had noted that one of his prime competitors, Western, was doing just that in reverse.

The issue that concerned Dean was weight. Dean was confident that he produced a better light-truck plow. But the shipping cost was considerable. Would a customer, i.e. a midwestern truck dealer, be able to cover the Fisher cost and compete with Western's home-grown competition? Research showed that the answer was a *yes*. Fisher offered a well-made and lasting plow whose quality could virtually offset the weight-price differential.

As of this day, Fisher Engineering's plant remains in Rockland, Maine. The firm was purchased in 1984 by its competitor, Western Products, headquartered in Milwaukee. Incidentally, Western changed its own name to Douglas Dynamics in 1968 and has subsequently further expanded its offerings by adding the Blizzard snowplow line.

It is noteworthy that several snowplow manufacturers have elected to diversify from their seasonal market (winter products) into truck accessories and lawn garden items, such as fertilizer/seed spreaders (spring and summer sellers). These lines have been accessed through acquisition. While the seasons are different, the method of sale, through local dealers, remains similar.

Thus far, our illustrations have focused on firms that produce and sell finished (end-use) products and services, but these illustrations apply to component producers as well.

Component manufacturers and product suppliers can diversify by promoting their capabilities with a limited investment with, typically, less risk than end-product providers can. Their "product" is their production equipment supported by their research and service knowledge.

A good example is a previously mentioned client of mine, Bixby International. Its president, Dan Rocconi, has designated four "platforms" of prospects. These platform categories (belting, construction, footwear, and orthopedics) represent definitive market groupings in which Bixby's coating and laminating capabilities effectively compete in (i.e. serve).

Dan feels that Bixby has achieved significant penetration in these four markets to the point that further corporate growth may be limited. Thus, he and his sales team regularly attend trade shows in other fields looking for end products that could be pursued as a new Bixby diversified growth-sourcing platform.

Another major form of new-market diversification is government-commercial (both ways: to and from). One of my most interesting studies involved a space-products supplier for NASA, a firm named AVCO (long since disappeared). AVCO developed and produced a high-tech thermal coating for domestic spacecraft in the 1970s. Visualizing an opportunity to enter the commercial building products market, AVCO engaged my services to investigate that opportunity.

Commercial buildings contain steel structural posts that, by law, must be coated with a fire-retardant material. Contractors currently use a relatively inexpensive spray coating. Shortly after this application has been approved by a building inspector, the wall is closed in by concrete, thus creating the structures' visible outer wall. Once this encasing process had been completed, no one can tell whether the spray coating still exists or has flaked off.

AVCO had an excellent product, one that would probably last as long as the building itself. As is often the case, the government-developed product was far more expensive than its competitive commercial counterpart. The cost-sensitive construction industry was not receptive to a better but much more expensive product. As soon as the coating product passed inspection and was sealed out of sight, its durability no longer became a factor.

An interesting sequel to this vignette follows. My study pointed out the pricing discrepancy, which should have ended the project idea. However, AVCO continued to commit research resources to this "opportunity." Apparently no one in the company wanted to take ownership of a failure! Perhaps, the project manager expected to be promoted before his project budget was rescinded.

Another difficulty that government suppliers have found in entering the commercial market is its culture. Military supply manufacturers function in a much different way from their commercial counterparts. It is very difficult for a new entrant to switch to the government market's culture. If the manufacturer wishes to try to produce the two types of products simultaneously, it had best establish a separate commercial division physically apart from the government manufacturing source.

My experience is that the two can't be successfully combined and produced in the same building or business quarters. One reason: quality levels are very different between commercial and government-produced goods. The government demands continued product performance with price secondary, while a consumer's selection is dictated by a delicate balance between price and performance.

Sales of commercial products *to* the government have a far better chance of success. the General Service Administration (GSA) schedule provides a map of potential domestic opportunities.

> *Tip: The key to selling to the government is price. Being the low bidder on a contract provides an entry point. Quality comes, but later.*

Firms open to diversification often fail to grasp and correctly assess new market opportunities. That's where market research can be an effective tool. One of my clients, Loctite Corporation, a supplier of adhesives to the consumer market, observed that sail panels, in the manufacturing process, were still being stitched together by hand—a time-consuming effort. My client correctly noted that stitching was laborious and opined that their adhesive product could temporarily hold the panels in place, thus improving the speed of stitching and reducing manufacturing costs.

Unfortunately, the proposed adhering process did not result in a significant offsetting labor savings and thus the idea was not pursued further.

Fast-forward to today's domestic textile market. In New England, few textile manufacturers have managed to counter the cost relocation advantages of overseas labor through technological innovation and greater efficiency. The Joseph Abboud Manufacturing Corporation of New Bedford, Massachusetts, offers an added key competitive advantage: rapid response to changing fashion requirements. Its president, Anthony Sapienza, was quoted in the *Boston Globe* (December 20, 2015) as saying, "In just four weeks, his factory can make a design change and have it in production. In China, pattern alterations alone would take weeks to complete, with their complete production process taking up to three months."

In a similar international involvement, but with a different outcome, I consulted for a Chinese firm that manufactures shoe components. They wished to diversify and produce their own end-product for the United States market with output (price and margin) they could control. Initially, they selected mattresses.

One might think that mattresses might be an ideal product for the Chinese to export (easily compacted and container-shipped). But local domestic (USA) suppliers offered individual customization and rapid direct shipping (lower dealer inventory cost), such that an overseas supplier was not able to compete. Note the similarities to the Abboud example, but with a different competitive outcome.

However, this Chinese manufacturer did identify a desirable product to sell in the United States. With the help of an international representative organization, my Chinese client has ended up manufacturing inexpensive metal bed frames for government institutions, namely the expanding United States correctional institution market!

What do these examples illustrate? Two interesting points. First, the important role of market research when pursuing a new market option. Second, the variety of ideas available that represent diversification opportunities.

Market Research

Areas for the would-be diversifier to examine closely:

- *Market expansion.* Is the market in question growing? At what rate? What segments are particularly promising? For example, the drug industry is expanding. Within that industry, the animal segment is doing particularly well. Within this segment, the pet field appears particularly opportune.

  Tip: An expanding market niche offers an array of in-depth buyer opportunities for entry by a new supplier.

- *Competition.* How entrenched are the current suppliers? Have they proved to be innovative in the diversifier's area of interest, or are they self-satisfied with their market position? How might they respond to a newcomer?

Tip: It often takes the established provider more time to react to this new competition than the innovator anticipates—an important safety factor for the competing diversifier.

- *Market pricing.* To what extent has prevailing industry pricing been assessed? Be aware of terms and conditions offered by competitors. Study their practices, both those "published" and applied (i.e., discounts, payment terms, etc.).

The Product Concept

Keep in mind that the diversifier will likely be required to modify their product, pricing, promotion, and distribution policies in tailoring them to a new market's requirements. Allow time and funds for this to happen.

Introducing A Product

Establishing a product or service in a new market represents a major challenge. Why would a buyer want to switch to a new product sold by an untested source? You, as a provider, have the potential to offer three competitive attributes: *price, quality,* and *service.* Let's examine each, but in reverse order of initial importance.

Service is not a feature that will help get you in the door of a new account for the simple reason that the customer is unlikely to experience its benefit until after several orders have been delivered or a difficulty has been resolved.

Quality (i.e., performance) provides a similar initial acceptance problem. Advertising and promotion can aid by encouraging the buyer to test your product, but again, the customer must first try your offering to determine its value.

That leaves *price.* This is the most frequently used technique to obtain entry into a new account. An initial discount of 10 percent may be inadequate. Fifteen percent could prove sufficient. Twenty percent is the standard opener and usually gets the purchasing agent's attention. A question is how long can the supplier afford to maintain such an attractive price. Food chains, for example, introduce a new item at a discount price for a set time-period. For retail product introductions, the supplier can, and often does, offer introductory-deal price discounts to both the retailer and, often, the consumer.

There is one other method of gaining entry-value, particularly, for an original equipment manufacturer. The seller may suggest that the buyer needs another (second or third) source as a backup in case a problem develops with the current supplier's production or delivery service. Oft-cited selling examples alluding to potential difficulties are fire or flooding. In this era of on-time delivery, such an argument can have sales validity.

Takeaways

It is particularly challenging for a company to expand into an established market. The features of quality and service may be pluses for the newcomer, but only if the buyers are unhappy with their current suppliers in either of these respects.

This leaves price. A 20 percent discount represents a good

opening gambit (for a predetermined time-period). Price promotions are helpful. Buy-back guarantees are often used in the retail trade, as are shelf space purchases. These represent methods by which the provider initially assumes the risks of the seller.

CHAPTER 8
Strategic Redeployment

Capabilities reinvention is the most challenging form of diversification. It poses the highest possible risk. Why, then, would a company elect to try it? Two reasons stand out. The first, and most common, is that a company's current product family is no longer relevant because the focal point of the "cloud of opportunity" has shifted. The second is that a company's owner seeks or has reason to try something new and different.

A firm's management often can anticipate obsolescence of its product offering. For example, ownership may observe a business decline in the offing and has no substitute as a replacement. On other occasions unforeseen, sudden events can create an untenable situation. Such events could include a competitive breakthrough (technical or service), a hurricane or flood, a military action that might alter demand and supply channels, or a severe recession. Large corporations may have a contingency plan, but small firms usually don't.

Lack of Relevancy

History is littered with companies who failed to attempt reinvention until it was virtually too late. The buggy whip represents the classic illustration of an unrecognized market shift. I previously mentioned Eastman Kodak and Polaroid. The influx of the technology market has provided an even stronger "wind for change" than that initially evidenced in the photographic field.

A more current example is Nokia, the Finnish cell phone giant of the early part of this century. As a *New York Times* article (November 30, 2015) notes, "Nokia was once the world's largest manufacturer of cell phones, with a market capitalization of close to $250 billion. Nokia failed to adapt to the fast rise of smartphones and eventually sold its faltering handset business to Microsoft. Now, attempting to remake itself once again, Nokia has turned to manufacturing the telecom equipment that powers the mobile networks of global carriers like Deutsche Telekom and China Mobile." Their newest attempt at reinvention involves a takeover of their Franco-American rival Alcatel-Lucent in a share-swap deal.

A related case is Samsung, currently the world's largest manufacturer of smartphones. It is now producing cancer drugs developed by Bristol-Myers Squibb Company. According to the *Wall Street Journal* (December 19, 2015), Samsung's goal is "to become the world's biggest contract manufacturer of biologic drugs by 2020."

Both these companies had projected limited long-term growth in their original fields. There is some synergy possible through their proposed strategy revision. They have positioned their corporate shell with their mass low-cost production resources as a capability for the pursuit of new mass markets. Time will tell whether their approach will succeed.

Moving closer to home, we have General Electric, a firm founded by Thomas Edison in 1892. Until recently, its offerings included electric light bulbs, refrigerators, and microwave ovens. Under its famous business leader Jack Welsh, it developed a major financial arm, GE Capital. His successor, Jeffrey Immelt, set out to change General Electric's essence. He is transforming this behemoth, a firm with market value of some $235 billion and three hundred thousand employees in 180 countries, into a "tech" focused equipment manufacturer.

Most everything about GE has changed. Most noticeable has been its headquarters move from the grassy vista of its Fairfield, Connecticut, campus to the Fort Point Channel area of Boston. It is now located in Boston's technically creative hub near Harvard, MIT, and numerous other universities—the center of innovative thought. No longer can GE be considered a staid, old manufacturing institution!

Recently, Procter and Gamble (my former employer) has come under fire from investors for not recreating itself in accordance with its customers' changes in buying habits. As noted in a *Wall Street Journal* article (November 1, 2016), Procter and Gamble's chief executive, David Taylor, eschews talk of reinvention. Although Procter and Gamble's organic growth has steadily declined over the past decade, Mr. Taylor prefers to "tighten the corporate belt" as opposed to altering the company's strategic composition. Let's see how this strategy plays out in the next several years.

On the service side, note the impact of Uber and Lyft on the taxi industry. The value of a taxi medallion has dropped precipitously as the need for this formal operating device has been lessened.

On smaller scale, Hamilton Thorne Company provides an example of the challenges of entering a new market with a promising new product. In 1975, Meg Spencer, a dynamic equestrian, "jumped" into the horse breeding market with a new product, the Equitainer. This device, engineered by Diarmaid Douglas Hamilton (a physicist, now Meg's husband), allowed equine and, later, bovine sperm to be transported from the stallion to the mare (for breeding purposes and increased conception rates) without the need, physically, to relocate the stud mare to her mate. This product changed the equine breeding world. It is allowed by all but the thoroughbred registry (which does not permit any artificial insemination).

Not content with acceptance in this niche market, Meg convinced Diarmaid to design a similar device for the reproductive toxicology field, the HMS IVOS analyzer, for the much larger human fertility market. Reportedly, this device was an instant success. However, in March 2001, the government changed regulations that favored the pharmaceutical companies, thus forcing Hamilton Thorne into other product areas. Playing in these "big leagues" was a step too big and a step too far for Meg and her company to pull off at that time.

Today, Hamilton Thorne has added a unique laser product line that fits into a microscope and is effectively used on embryos in the infertility market and stem cell research field. This product line is regarded as the leader in the field worldwide.

In situations where an owner wishes to try a completely new venture, there are typically two noticeable factors that can contribute to realizing success. The first is that the owner has some familiarity with the new business product or service. This knowledge-involvement is often acquired through a sport or hobby. The second is that the owner is financially astute, i.e., a "numbers person."

An analogy that illustrates this point appears in the field of human anatomy. The composition of a person's blood is one of the first tests a doctor uses to diagnose a serious illness. That is because a person's blood flows throughout the entire body and thus carries and conveys vital life signs. Similarly, "numbers" are the lifeblood of a company, as they extend from sales to net profit. A financially oriented individual has the capacity to understand the essence of most any type of organization, whether it is a for-profit or a non-profit firm.

Two success-factor examples illustrate the wide divergence this form of diversification can take. The first relates to the individual's hobby. Bill Stewart, a friend from Maine, began his career on the trading floor of the New York Stock Exchange and advanced through the investment ranks to a point where he took his company public and then sold it for several million dollars.

With an altruistic goal of helping the Vietnamese people to get back on their financial feet (and to make some money in the process), he purchased a large, vine-overgrown dairy farm in Vietnam. First, he switched to vegetable production, but then he further developed this business into a producer of flowers that are now distributed throughout the Far East. His son-in-law has facilitated this transformation.

Subsequently, the company vertically diversified by opening retail floral outlets (shops) in China, Japan, and other Asian countries. The firm's corporate office is in Hong Kong. Bill's primary residence is in tax-friendly Bermuda. He summers in Maine and became a large-boat owner. To thwart a local land developer's acquisition, he bought a local boatyard. This acquisition came packaged with a restaurant. Bill then acquired a reliable manager, and now he simply monitors the boatyard's books.

The other successful example is a recent acquaintance, Thomas Peterfly, a Hungarian by birth who made his fortune (firm: Interactive Brokers) by developing a probability-distribution model for trading stock options. As a domestic hedge against the government asset privation he experienced as a child when his country was taken over by Germans and then subjugated by the Russians, Thomas acquired a large sheep farm in New Zealand. He followed this by acquiring a cattle ranch in Florida. Talk about diversification! His motivation for diversification may best be described as a dual-faceted political safety net.

Thomas monitors performance of his far-flung enterprises through their financial records. Obviously, he has confidence in the general managers responsible for their operations.

> Tip: It is essential, in any such diversified acquisition,
> that the owner invest the necessary time to acquire
> a responsible general manager.

See note 1. In neither of these cases was the owner driven by a compelling desire for monetary growth. They had both already made their fortunes.

Apart from these two personal examples, this form of reinvention provides one of the greatest risk methods of growth. Two difficulties stand out:

1. Lack of ownership's understanding of the functionality of the new venture.
2. Inability of management to project the transition time from concept to implementation accurately.

EnerNoc Corporation, a fifteen-year-old NYSE firm, in which I initially invested, began experiencing financial challenges in trying to grow its energy grid management operation as the complexities of the energy field multiplied. It is attempting to reinvent itself as a provider of energy intelligence software (EIS) sold directly to major corporations. Obtaining market acceptance of this new service is proving to be quite a challenge for EnerNoc, as the decline in its stock price attests.

Just recently, EnerNoc was sold for $300 million. It never was effective in defining itself in its diversified role. As its CEO, Tim Healy, stated, "It's a complex business for investors to understand." That goes for the customers as well.

Takeaway

The opportunities for profitable growth through reinvention are, at best, slim. Without a doubt, the most successful reinvention strategy is to acquire an established, privately-owned company in an expanding market—one with solid management in place. Such companies are hard to find and expensive to acquire as equity investors will attest.

> *Tip: In the due-diligence review of the acquisition candidate, the would-be buyer should try to ascertain the defining reason(s) that the current ownership decided to list the company for sale. Often the stated reason doesn't tell the full story.*

Note 1. Most of these acquirers tend to retain the current staff (owner or general manager) for a six-month to two-year transition period. Keep in mind that it is unlikely that a replacement GM will have the commitment or financial support to institute any significant diversified growth program, as he or she may lack the personal involvement of the new owners.

CHAPTER 9
Odds and Ends

Vertical Integration

This book would not be complete without discussing other-than-horizontal diversification. The most common such form of diversification is *vertical integration*. I have included all remaining forms of diversification into this category.

Vertical movement <u>upward</u> (i.e., adding a better-quality and pricier product or service line) is rare. A novel, recent example of planned upward integration is Howard Schultz, the CEO of Starbucks, departing from that position to introduce a program to build high-end coffee shops (charging up to twelve dollars per cup) aimed at refreshing the Starbucks brand as it encounters increased competition from both specialty roasters and mass coffee purveyors such as Dunkin' Donuts.

Vertical movement <u>downward</u> is a more frequently encountered form of vertical integration. The prime motivator of ownership, when considering downward mobility, is cost savings: does it save the company money? Equally important, will it facilitate a price reduction to the customer and thus enhance the product's sales appeal?

Most frequently, downward mobility consists of absorbing (in house) subcontracted product delivery. This is commonly identified as a key element within supply chain management (SCM). The prime advantages of this form of diversification are twofold: reducing shipping and handling costs and improving reliability of delivery. There are, typically, a minimum of three distribution levels involved in the steps between the producer and the customer:

1. The corporate warehouse
2. The distributor
3. The retailer

These steps can, all or in part, be outsourced by the producer. Or they can be brought in-house—an illustration of the potential of vertical diversification.

A prime example of this downward diversification-absorption is Amazon's experimental delivery system—by drone, no less! Their goal is to meet customer demand for more orders delivered faster to the consumer's front door. Currently, they are investing heavily in warehouse expansion as part of a downward diversification effort, achieved by adding their own direct-shipping capabilities (see Chapter 6 for prior discussion of Amazon's efforts in this regard).

This delivery example simultaneously illustrates two levels of vertical diversification: warehousing expansion and potential delivery directly to the customer (they can be one and the same—see the appendix section). In Amazon's case, the initial costs of this program were substantial, dramatically impacting their earnings in 2016. This earnings impact was exacerbated by their Prime membership program, which offered free delivery for a ninety-nine-dollar annual fee—a tweaked form of diversification in and of itself. More recent comments on Amazon appear in the appendix as this extraordinary firm continues to expand with its octopus-like tentacles.

Nike represents another example of a major firm that plans

to emphasize direct (sneaker) sales to the customer, as opposed to relying on the distributor as a middle-man between manufacturer and customer. The consumer will be encouraged to buy through Nike's app or from Nike stores, such as their recently opened test store in New York City. These direct outlets will feature limited-edition sneaker products. This is another prominent example of vertical (i.e. downward) diversification.

Tesla has stepped past the third-party retail distribution phase employed by other automobile manufactures. It sells its cars *directly* to the customer through factory showrooms.

On a smaller scale, Night Shift Brewing has launched its own beer distribution company, aptly named Night Shift Distributing. Currently, this distributing arm is configured to deliver Night Shift beer to bars and restaurants, but, in addition, they plan to deliver other brands from up to twenty-five craft beer makers to retailers across Massachusetts and beyond. Here we have an example of both vertical and horizontal diversification being pursued simultaneously. A multifaceted strategy!

Supply Chain Management

A corollary to this vertical integration concept is the absorption of outsourced processing services (which might conceivably have had an in-house origin). They could include *component manufacture, assembly manufacture,* or *packaging.* This component venue might involve a multi-product process extending through several stations. Other services that could be brought in-house might include accounting (bookkeeping), training, etc. However, these illustrations take us beyond the parameters of this text.

Partnerships

There are two kinds of partnerships: *investment* and *strategic alliance*. What I refer to as an *investment* partnership is one in which a company buys a minority interest in another firm for strategic reasons. Typically, the investing company will position one or more (depending on the significance of the investment) of its representatives on the board of directors of the investee.

A *strategic alliance* occurs when two companies arrange to work together for their mutual advantage. For example, Wal-Mart Stores, seeking to reduce its electronic payment costs, has allied itself with J. P. Morgan Chase Banking's capabilities by offering Chase Pay as a vehicle for Walmart shoppers to pay for items purchased on the Internet and via its app. In 2016 Walmart acquired Jet.com as a vehicle for enhancing its e-commerce toehold to sync its on-line and in-store sales offerings.

Diversified Shrinkage

When a company diversifies away from its core competency, it increases risk. Often, such a strategy is pursued when a new CEO takes over, as illustrated by Jeff Immelt's actions at GE which have resulted in a substantial devaluation of the company's stock price.

Financial constraints may dictate that a company sell off a portion of its assets to survive or meet financial projections. *Keep in mind that such actions realign the strategic balance of the company.* General Motors announced that it plans to cull some of its Cadillac dealers, for example. General Electric has announced plans to divest it light bulb manufacturing arm, its original business, as mentioned in the previous chapter.

Takeaways

Diversification may best be pictured as a coat of many colors. Besides a myriad of horizontal expansion options, it can include vertical elements as well as outsourced-capabilities absorption. This further illustrates the multitude of diversification strategy options that are available to management.

CHAPTER 10
Mix and Match

This book's presentation, thus far, has separated the *products or services* and the *markets* categories. However, the real world doesn't function quite that simply. Reality is, in fact, a more fluid concept. Two such categories are headlined and then discussed below:

- *Simultaneous diversification efforts.* Companies often elect to pursue several approaches concurrently.
- *Associated capabilities.* Ancillary corporate attributes can play a role in developing a diversification strategy.

Simultaneous Diversification Efforts

Approaches can range widely from enhancing multiple current offerings to acquisitions in either a current or a new market. While such a multiplex strategy can accelerate revenue growth, it may create excessive risk and certainly will have an impact on both Manpower and financial resources.

> *Tip: A certain level of expertise is required in assessing and pursuing, specifically, new industry ventures. The owner should beware of broadening the program beyond the capabilities of the project implementer, particularly when a single individual remains responsible for a multitude of existing activities.*

Associated Capabilities

This is a catch-all category. It includes factors other than simple diversification into new products or markets. These factors can include *production resources* (equipment and capacity), *owner interests* (avocational and vocational), *competitive growth/profit opportunities,* and *available capital.* Several examples illustrate the complexity of this multifaceted mix-and-match concept.

Acorn Manufacturing Company

Acorn is a third-generation manufacturer of early American builders' hardware. It produces builders hardware for such products as doors, cabinets, window shutters, garage door hardware, and bathroom accessories. The firm also produces square-cut nails for masonry floors and restoration projects. All these products were originally marketed through hardware stores directly, through a network of independent sales representatives, and more recently, via the Internet.

When Eric DeLong took over the business from his father, these products were produced from forged iron and malleable-iron castings. Like the Model T Ford, they were offered primarily in the color black.

Eric realized that his niche-market product category was and would increasingly be subject to overseas competition from, likely, China. As sales eroded, he turned to God for guidance (Eric is a deeply religious person). This guidance manifested itself in opening his mind to the creation of new possibilities. As Eric told me, "If an opportunity presents itself, I'll find a way to do it. Never say no."

Tip: Opportunity and timing are not natural bed partners, but if you keep the receptivity door open, the appropriate timing may become evident.

In his first significant diversification step, he added a line of floor-ventilation grates. This market suggestion was provided by his casting supplier, who said he saw an opportunity for Acorn to compete price-wise with a staid domestic manufacturer. Eric developed a Chinese supply source, thus gaining an initial launch price advantage on his competitor (the competitor ultimately responded by switching his production to an overseas manufacturer).

Next, Eric acquired, from an inventor, an undeveloped line of decorative baseboard heater-covers and end-caps made from extruded and cast aluminum, primarily used for forced hot water systems (i.e., radiators).

Then, responding to a "feeler" from the owner of Tremont Nail, who had decided to sell because of overseas competition, Eric expressed an interest. While Eric knew nothing about cut nails and their market parameters he did have a long relationship with the Tremont Nail Company. Both Acorn and Tremont sold into the restoration market and marketed their lines through the same *Company Store* catalog.

Not long after purchasing Tremont, Eric was approached by Wheeling LaBelle, the only other cut-nail manufacturer still producing in the United States. Wheeling LaBelle was manufacturing only masonry cut nails. Eric learned that the primary markets were Puerto Rico and other Caribbean countries that use masonry products in household construction. He also learned that there was competition from China, but even so, business could be gained through superior quality and on-time shipments. After two years, several trips, and months of negotiations, a purchase-sale agreement was made.

With great effort (two years in the making), he transported Tremont's giant (half the size of a football field) nail and packaging manufacturing machinery from North Carolina to Massachusetts. It took Eric an additional year to get this machinery up and running.

Tip: The pursuit of one opportunity often opens doors to others.

Soon thereafter, Eric was approached by the sole European cut-nail manufacturer (located in Glasgow, Scotland), who was also interested in retiring. Eric bought his machine (an asset purchase) and had it shipped to this country. Now, from the United States, he services the entire Western market. The only remaining wooden-nail competitor is located in India.

In hindsight, Acorn appears to have evolved a growth strategy. It ties together the firm's manufacturing capability (metal stamping and painting), its overall experience in the hardware market, and its ability to exploit niche markets that larger competitors no longer find profitable.

One of the best examples of "mix and match" was described in Chapter 4: the American Automobile Association. While their diversified product selections may not have been pursued simultaneously, they certainly are numerous and varied.

Another example has occurred in the breakfast market. A consumer decline in morning cereal appetites has triggered a diversified response from the major producers. As an illustration, PostHoldings, which sells Grape Nuts, now additionally sells eggs and protein shakes. Kellogg has put more fruit in its Special K Red Berry cereal. General Mills has stripped genetically modified ingredients and gluten from Cheerios and reportedly plans to remove all artificial flavors and colors from its cereals by 2018.

Takeaways

There are a variety of ways that a company can grow using a diversification strategy. Depending on the degree of urgency, some firms will elect to pursue several diversification options simultaneously.

In cases where programs are pursued in unison, the risk increases, in proportion, to the number and type of plans selected. The element of risk will be either enhanced or (sometimes) lessened by the multiplicity of concurrent diversification ventures. An overall risk-management assessment program becomes essential.

CHAPTER 11

The Road Ahead

Sailing into the Future

The past is, probably, our best guide to the future, but we often ignore the wisdom of yesteryear. Somehow, our immediate past no longer seems relevant. However, history tends to repeat itself in long-term cycles. So, be alert!

Having offered the above observation, let's examine what impact future events might have on our diversification plans. After all, we are constantly being schooled in *forward thinking*.

The future is arriving, perhaps faster than we can absorb. In his new book, *Thank You for Being Late*, Tom Friedman states the world "is being driven by simultaneous accelerations in technology, globalization, and climate change, all interacting with one another." That's the backdrop for the long-term, but retain those thoughts. It never hurts to be moving with the current.

Diversification, typically (excepting in corporate reinvention), is considered an ancillary activity as related to a company's main business strategic thrust. As such it can, and perhaps is, initially viewed as having a somewhat momentary and transitory role in the essence of a company's structure. In my admittedly limited simplistic listing of future business trends, I have established three categories, starting with the most immediate.

- *Current impact*. Those chronicled below are in an evolving and fluid state. Thus, they must be noted, but with great caution as we are at the midpoint of their impact and thus lack perspective on their ultimate influence:

1. The Internet. It increasingly influences our daily lives in a multitude of different, expanding ways. Our iPhone is an example. From a broad range of news media, we are constantly being exposed to new app products, new medical discoveries, and new inventions.

2. Our government. Shifts in state and national policies impacting spending (education, medical research, local regulations, etc.) occur constantly—when least expected. Global events unexpectedly occur that impact us.

    The federal government has recently announced that it will be significantly increasing military spending and is planning to increase tariffs for imported aluminum and steel. But, in the latter case, steep duties and quotas could impact domestic manufacturers that have become dependent on imported metals.

3. Fads. What is in favor one day is taboo the next, particularly in the retail field. Clothing fashions are a prime example. Tastes in food and wine are another.

- *Trends and Shifts.* These represent subtle changes in our lives. As such, they often go unnoticed until their impact is upon us. Astute business executives are aware of these changes and build them into their growth strategies.

    Three major corporate examples of slowly emerging trends come to mind:

1. A subtle shift that you may not have noticed, but that affects you as a food shopper, is that the top food brands are losing shelf space to fresh foods, prepared hot meals, and local, healthy upstart products.

2. More specifically, Procter and Gamble has noted that their share of Downy Fabric Softener has been declining steadily for the past ten years. In fact, the younger generation of consumers often lacks knowledge of this product-concept entirely. The need for a fabric softener has been negated by stronger fabrics, improved washing machine technology, and modern detergents.

3. In repositioning General Electric for long-term growth (see Chapter 8), Jeffrey Immelt, GE's former CEO, quietly shifted his firm's strategic growth from machinery design and manufacture to software with sophisticated sensors to control its GE engines and other types of machinery.

- *Tectonic plate-like movement.* Rapid-change categories, as mentioned earlier (e.g., fads and technology) may not have a momentary impact on your diversification plans. Nevertheless, slower-evolving shifts should be identified, if for no other reason than to complete our list and thus contribute to the framework of this chapter. Some examples:

1. The ageing of our population. The average median age of our domestic workforce is increasing slowly, but steadily. According to the Bureau of Labor Statistics, in

1994, it was 37.7, in 2004 it was 40.3, and in 2015 it was 42.3 years of age.

2. The method by which our office workforce functions. More employees now work from home (relying on modern forms of communication). The Bureau of Labor Statistics confirms this upward trend of some or all workers working from home—19 percent in 2003 to 24 percent in 2015; longer time-off is given for maternity leaves of absence; and corporate loyalty has fallen off significantly. Turnover has become more routine.

Tip: The prime factor in employee retention is the relationship between the employee and his or her boss.

3. The weather. Whether we accept it or not, we have all heard about global warming. Three noticeable factors: our weather is getting warmer, albeit gradually; severe storms are less frequent, but more powerful; and flooding in certain geographic areas is more prevalent.

4. The shifting sands of change. The annual sales of bottled water now exceed that of soda. The bottled-water market, driven by health and wellness concerns, now is over $21 billion in this country.

5. Evolution. Remember the days of our childhood, when our parents would take us to the local bookstore to select an appropriate age-level book? Then along came the Barnes and Noble block-sized chain outlets, and

the corner bookstore disappeared. Now Amazon has appeared and is bankrupting the Barnes and Nobles of the world.

Takeaways

While the latter of these listed categories are unlikely to have any immediate impact on a company's emerging diversification strategy, they should be assessed when considering diversified growth options. It is best to be moving with the current, however slow.

> *Tip: Good news. Diversified business programs you initiate likely will be impactful for <u>longer</u> than you might expect—be aware.*

Who can tell? The future of your company may become the present faster than you anticipate. Your growth strategy could end up tracking the path of your diversified strategies.

CHAPTER 12
Opportunities

We have broadly covered the numerous and varied options that diversification might include. Perhaps a check list might prove helpful, thus pinpointing the many forms of diversification available to the reader. Over thirty basic diversification options are offered.

Horizontal Diversification

Enhancements (estimated risk factor minimal: 10–20 percent)

- *Packaging.* Alter appearance of both product and outer package.
- *Pricing.* Offer "specials"; adjust discounts and payment terms.
- *Product.* Improve performance; add features (new bells and whistles).
- *Promotion.* Change advertising message by better targeting market, add examples to web page, introduce a special price (offer) to marketplace, upgrade warrantee period, run a sales contest.

New products, current market (estimated risk factor moderate: 50 percent)

Start by developing a list of new product ideas. Contact sources:

- Current staff.
- Suppliers (raw, material, component, services, etc.).
- Key customers.
- Sales staff (your own and independent representatives).
- Trade association executives and other experts.
- Trade magazines and seminars.
- Friends and associates (including your mate).

New product sources (some options):

- Upgrade product or service offering; improve features.
- Add a technically improved product line.
- Acquire related products to broaden current line.
- Develop partnership agreement (to take on other products).
- Duplicate industry leaders' most successful products or services.

New markets (estimated risk factor high: 60–75 percent)

- Expand geographically (regionally and overseas).
- Market to United States government (GSA).
- Pursue undeveloped niche markets.
- Expand into higher and/or lower ends of current market

Pure diversification (estimated risk factor very high: 75–90 percent)

- Acquire another ongoing business (for lowest risk, a related one).
- Change the nature of the existing (core) business. Track your "Cloud of Opportunity."
- Use imagination to visualize solutions to market need; then pursue if viable.

Vertical Diversification or Integration

Upward

- Introduce a "premium" or fancier model.
- Provide preferential products or services (example: airlines).

Downward: Create your own warehouse operation

- Bypass distributors. Sell directly from the warehouse to the retailer.
- Sell directly to the customer, bypassing independent retailers.

Other: SCM (supply chain management) and additional options

- Bring (or bring back) in-house outsourced functions, such as accounting, component manufacturing, and training.
- Affiliate or partner with like-minded companies in sales or distribution.

Acquisitions

This book would be remiss if it didn't discuss acquisitions as a vehicle for diversification. This strategy offers several advantages, chief among which is that it provides the buyer with a relatively known entity with a documented past.

Specific plusses include the following:

- Broaden corporate product or service market reach
- Gain more efficient allocation of sales and promotion costs
- Consolidate overhead expenses (administration, distribution, etc.)
- Build revenue and assets on your balance sheet

However, *seldom does the acquisition live up to the buyer's value expectations*. Research has noted that most acquisitions fail to achieve management's anticipated positive outcome. Let's examine some of the issues.

Securing the Acquisition

Good acquisitions are *extremely hard to find*. The supply of desirable candidates is far more than offset by the number of would-be buyers. Consequently, the law of supply and demand dictates that the purchaser ends up overpaying.

For mid-sized corporate buyers, spinoffs from larger companies represent a frequently accessed source of candidates. Such candidates are relatively smaller operations that no longer fit their parents' strategic growth plans or are no longer geographically positioned advantageously.

Tip: Initiate and develop contact with parent com-
panies of potential spinoffs well before the spinoff
option is publicized to minimize competition. The
early bird gets the emerging worm.

Should you elect to pursue the acquisition-diversification path, there are several cautionary words of advice, which I have grouped into three categories: *planning, the search,* and *integration.*

Planning

Planning is a vital phase, often overlooked by decision makers in their haste to pursue an opportunity. In the ever-more-rapidly growing and turbulent political/business world in which we function, planning is a key to reducing risk and thus maximizing opportunity.

A backup plan is of value as well. Often, planned activities don't materialize with the anticipated outcome.

Some key questions that should be addressed:

- Why is the targeted acquisition *really* being offered for sale? What are the seller's full range of motivations?
- What is the underlying reason that the target company is being placed on the market at this time? If it has been available for sale for a lengthy period, either the price is too elevated or it has some other major problem.
- What is the seller's market position? Has the firm grown over the last three to five years? What is the likelihood of further growth? Who are its major competitors?

- What is your relationship with the seller? If it an individual owner, will he or she be retained, and if so, under what conditions and for how long?

- Who are or will be your key staff members involved in the transition and thereafter? Are they currently aware of the pending acquisition? What is their honest personal reaction to the sale?

- Who will manage the acquisition once the sale is complete? How will the manager's compensation package be structured versus what he or she is currently receiving? In what form will he or she be compensated?

- How do you plan to meld the acquired company (leadership and employees) into your business, assuming their business philosophy differs from yours (which is likely)? A critical element is the acquired company's staff—both management and workers. In addition, consider utilization of the acquired company's equipment (manufacturing and office). Finally, note the company's outstanding obligations and commitments, both short- and long-term. An integration timetable will help.

- How might the key customers (the top five to ten) react? On the positive side, they may welcome a change in supplier, particularly if current deliveries are not timely. Or they may, adversely, embrace the overtures of a long-pursuing competitor. This acquisition assessment is very difficult to make, as the firm being acquired may not want to have the word of their pending sale leak out, as it may jeopardize their business if the acquisition fails to materialize.

Tip: With the permission of the prospective seller, you should contact the two or three principal customers (the major accounts).

The Search

As previously noted, the search process can be lengthy. Several approaches are commonly employed. They include the following:

- Soliciting input from the owner, principal, or senior management team (directors included)
- Assigning an employee to this task, either on a full-time or part-time basis.
- Engaging an outsider or mergers and acquisitions specialist. A specialist typically charges either a results commission or on a fee-plus-results basis. Both approaches have advantages and drawbacks.

    Since acquisitions are such a difficult and risk-oriented method of growth, I have elected to add material directly from Adam Chase, CEO of Chase Corporation, thus sharing his experience on targeting acquisition candidates.

    1. What does the buyer bring to the transaction to enhance the target's performance?
    2. Does the target provide access to new markets and technology?
    3. Would the acquisition improve corporate attractiveness to current and prospective customers?
    4. Can acquiring the target change the competitive dynamics within the industry, thus allowing the

buyer to enhance profitability? Would there be additional acquisition add-on opportunities?

5. Will the deal enhance the buyer's earnings? Will it support other relevant financial performance measures?

6. What is the strength of the target's talent base, if its existing management resources are to be acquired?

It is often advisable to acquire *just* the assets of the seller's company. If you are purchasing the entire operation, including facilities, be particularly wary of hidden charges—the most common of which are lawsuits (existing or pending) and EPA concerns (below-surface ground contamination).

Integrating the Acquisition

The overall integration process might best be categorized as *cultural transformation* for both the acquirer and, particularly, for the firm being acquired. Viewed from the seller's perspective, some important concerns are these:

- Has the general manager (or COO) of the seller been fully appraised of the actual sale details? What was or is the general manager's reaction?

- Have the employees who are to be retained been informed of the transfer timetable? Will it involve additional commuting time, and thus travel expense, for them? How are they going to be introduced to their new colleagues? Where will they fit into their new corporate structure, from both a reporting and social standpoint?

- For employees destined to be released, how will their termination be handled (compensation and exit timing)? Will they be asked to sign a non-compete agreement?

  Tip: In most cases, an immediate separation is advisable. At the time of termination, make certain to demand the car keys and computer (if company property) from the released employee.

Takeaways

We have examined vertical and tangential diversification options. However, the major focus has been on horizontal opportunities. Besides including the concept of tweaking the current product mix, the horizontal diversification category encompasses product line extensions, with prime emphasis on new product and new market diversification.

We have thus broadly covered the diversification waterfront.

CHAPTER 13

Optimizing Return on Investment

Most likely added profitability is the ultimate corporate goal in implementing a diversification strategy. Let us examine some of the most significant maximization opportunities in this respect

> *Tip: The producer of the acquired products or services may not have recently analyzed their internal or external costs and thus, may not be pursuing the most efficient operating and marketing methods.*

Internal Costs

- Overhead savings are the first place to look for an expense reduction. If the new venture can be added to an existing employee's responsibilities, then labor cost is minimal. A cautionary note: the additional responsibilities may be excessive for the employee to manage effectively.
- Vendor efficiencies may be realized. These could be from outside suppliers, ranging from component manufacturers to accounting or legal services. For an acquisition, *every* cost item should be reviewed with an eye to reducing the amount of the expenditure. *It is unlikely that the target company has recently conducted such an audit.*

Market-Driven Opportunities

- *The customer.* In absorbing a company or product line the acquirer might start by examining the products or services offered by the new company's prime competitors. The acquirer should speak to both the current sales staff and its customers themselves. A market research study could be used as an additional information source; consider employing business school students on a project basis if cost is a consideration.
- *Product innovations.* Either directly or certainly indirectly, technological enhancements can contribute to marketing efficiencies. The *direct* portion relates to product innovations. The *indirect* relates to the vendor side. A further point of information -as noted in the MicroMedia example (chapter 5)- be careful that a competitor is not preparing to upstage your market entry with a new product of their own.

Takeaways

Efficiencies in cost and marketing controls should help accelerate the return on investment. *It is impractical to budget such savings in the original plan; just use them to offset unanticipated expenses.*

CHAPTER 14
Implementation

As a market-responsive business executive, you should continually reflect on the potential opportunities afforded by adopting a strategy of diversification, not just when the situation calls for action.

Are you currently set to "pull-the-trigger"? When thus prepared, make sure you are really - *ready*. Presumably you have squared away (1) financing, (2) staff responsibilities, and (3) current business obligations. You have selected the one (or more) diversification concepts you now intend to pursue and launch—so let's get started.

Here is a sequential checklist of activities to assist you in achieving success with your diversification program(s). This checklist is divided into three key components: *plan, execution,* and *follow-on.*

But first, two critical admonitions:

1. Your checklist should be formalized to maximize success. By *formalized,* I mean *put in writing.* Likely, that is a given for the management of any company of size, but it should also apply to small, privately owned firms as well. Committing this document to writing forces you to think through the details of your plan, thus enhancing success.
2. The first two components (planning and execution) should be completed in *full.* No skimping! This also is a necessary step if risk is to be minimized and the desired return realized.

The Plan

This section should cover, as a minimum:

1. A carefully crafted summary statement featuring both diversification goals and objectives. An attachment should include income projections (for three years minimum): revenues and expenses, cash requirements, and anticipated payback (maximum three-year break-even point, with a five-year return on investment).

2. A short commentary as to how the diversification plan meshes with your corporate growth strategies, which, hopefully, are already committed to writing.

3. Comments as to how you and your key staff members intend to realize both the overall corporate diversification goal and their individual staff responsibilities in attaining this goal: i.e., such factors as timing, manpower commitment, progress, performance measurement, etc. This section is designed to make you and your staff aware of the expectations required to achieve the desired goals.

4. The identification of the risk elements involved and managed. The likelihood (percentage chance) of each risk issue occurring should be noted. Comments as to how any emerging problems might be addressed should be included.

5. The launch plan should be spelled out. It should start with the pretest phase (increasing in relative importance to the complexity of the diversification venture) and then move on to the market (customer) preparation, concluding with the launch itself (promotion).

6. A post-launch program should be envisioned. This would cover the first three-month period following the diversification program implementation. It would conclude with a review of the results versus the original plan (revenues, costs, and other results).

The Execution

This section should provide, in detail, the elements proposed in "The Plan." Steps involved would include the following:

1. Designation of personnel (including the implementation team) to review the plan and establish specific goals (sales and expense budgets) and a timetable for execution.
2. Management and team discussions as to the corporate opportunities that this diversification venture would afford the company and the risks involved—i.e., a reward-risk review. *The focal starting-point for each discussion should be the target customer.*
3. Some form of test-market program for validating the viability of this project—a beta test.
4. A review of how this diversification effort might be seamlessly integrated into the existing sales effort.
5. An understanding of who (which team members) will do what, how much extra time they should be budgeted for each phase, and how the program participants will be compensated.
6. Scheduling and implementation of a focused key-account customer/prospect program. *Their initial acceptance of the diversification project is critical.*

7. Involvement in integrating the diversification program into the acquirer's business operation. This would include its "delivery system" (the sales *and* distribution components).
8. Construction of an internal and external support network—the latter would encompass vendor integration.
9. The preparation and execution of a performance tracking system.

The Follow-On

If the two previous sections ("The Plan" and "The Execution") are effectively implemented, then this section is relegated to monitoring performance. This step should be pursued diligently for an agreed time period, with review sessions conducted periodically.

Additional Reflections

In concluding this chapter, I would like to restate, and thus underscore, several previously mentioned issues. So here goes:

The customer. Who or what is the *most* essential element in any diversification program? *It's the ultimate beneficiary.* He or she is the key to realizing success in any growth-oriented diversification effort.

> *Tip: Remember, all "marketing" begins with the customer.*

Without a customer, you don't have a business. Customer focus is critically important.

Make sure you *listen to the customer.* Identify his or her require-ments. If you are expanding into a new market, learn all you can about the customer and his or her desires and needs. Furthermore, if you are buying all or part of a business, your first priority is to retain its existing customer base, especially key accounts, as they generate the majority of the business you will be acquiring.

Two key words in the sales lexicon for retaining existing cus-tomers and marketing to new prospects are designated buyer *needs* and seller-offered *benefits.*

- *Needs.* As mentioned previously, for the ultimate purchaser to switch suppliers or convert to a new supply source, he or she must have a motivating need (price, delivery, and cus-tomer service are the most commonly offered incentives). It is the seller's responsibility to identify and communicate this need. If that cannot be realized, then this buyer should not be considered a legitimate end prospect.
- *Benefits.* The purchaser's needs are the critical element and forerunner to a benefits-oriented selling process. The most important selling benefits (see above) should be hammered home through repeated emphasis by the salesperson or in the sales message.

Customer retention. As previously discussed, in an acquisition, how do you, the acquirer, retain the target company's customers? Answer: by contacting these existing customers as soon as stra-tegically practical with a message of reassurance. Inform them that the service you intend to provide will be *superior* to what they have recently been receiving. Also, solicit their opinions on further improvements they might suggest.

Tip: Asking advice is both productive in gathering ideas and an excellent selling strategy.

Core customers (the largest 20 percent) should be contacted personally (by visit or telephone), the balance (the other 80 percent) with at least two postal mailings (not e-mails).

Seamless integration. Obviously, you want your diversification program to be successful. To qualify as successful, it must, as the renowned Harvard Business School professor Benjamin Shapiro noted, be blended into the company from *strategic, organizational, cultural, tactical,* and *innovative* standpoints. In other words, the diversification effort should meld into the parent company so that a seamless (and beneficial) fit is achieved as quickly as possible.

Results. Concluding the successful integration of a diversification strategy is measured in profitability." As a start in achieving this goal, you should separate the diversification program from the balance of the corporate sales effort and then track its individual performance numbers—*sales, gross profit,* and *net profit*—at least initially. You should also monitor its investment payback. Does it reach plan? If it fails to do so, then why?

Test market. It is always advisable to sample a product or service before committing to its introduction. As an illustration, when on vacation, we typically will put a toe or foot in the water before jumping in for a swim, thus assessing the temperature. That same principle holds true in pursuing a new venture. Admittedly, it is not always possible to sample a diversification opportunity without violating the seller's confidences, but every effort should be made to do so.

Tip: The more you learn about the diversification opportunity in advance, the more you will reduce your ultimate risk.

The introduction. The actual launch date is an important rallying point for both corporate personnel and would-be customers. Thus, it warrants further comment. Picture the launch as the neck of a shapely hourglass. The top section is filled with planning activities, which funnel into the launch. The bottom part spreads out from the launch date to form an expanding and ongoing marketing effort.

The launch activities (the actual introduction is frequently held at a trade fair) will likely include a variety of pre-planned programs, such as some combination of these:

- Press release
- Targeted Internet promotion
- Sampling to key customers and prospects
- Invitations to and/or personal visits with the "best" prospects
- A grand opening event preceded by a night-before-launch "pep rally"
- Flyers and giveaway mementos for all guests

Continuing Feedback. Don't neglect to track the results. Modify the marketing launch program as needed to assure continued success. As an executive involved with the food giant McDonald's recently said, "Everyone needs to reinvent to stay relevant."

Takeaways

This chapter provides you with a review of the most critical of the considerations you should consider when developing and pursuing a plan to grow through diversification.

Admittedly, some of these comments are redundant, but they are presented in such a way as to enable you to create a base to help prepare your own checklist of key issues to monitor (see Notes section).

CHAPTER 15
Concluding Comments

There you have it—a compendium of observations about diversification. We have identified basic and interrelated *horizontal, vertical,* and *tangential* options. You, the reader, have been exposed to a wide range of diversification situations, including product and program modifications, new markets, new products, and multiple combinations thereof. Examples of recent and recognizable events have been interspersed throughout the text to stimulate your imagination, with practical tips frequently inserted.

Currently, you may be comfortable in adapting to and evolving with the twists and turns of your current basic market strategy. Fine. If your company has grown thus far without employing a diversification scenario, so be it. But there are several reasons to consider pursuing such a developmental plan *now*. Three come to mind:

- Decelerating growth rate is appearing in the market segments you now serve. Current opportunities may not meet your long-range strategic expansion objectives. Eventually you will, most likely, exhaust existing growth limit.
- A desire for accelerated, continued-revenue growth that is unachievable through your present product and market mix.
- A perceived opportunity to broaden your corporate reach within the sales and profitability framework of acceptable cost and risk.

What might be your final takeaways from this book in establishing a practical diversification strategy for your firm that embodies minimal risk? These represent a checklist of the issues that I explore with my seminar participants:

1. Be aware of the timely shifting sands of your current marketplace that form the foundation of your business model. Diversification represents a growth option. Typically, it is fueled either by *opportunity* or *necessity*.

2. Consider the ramifications of embarking on a diversification program. Assess your *time, availability, funding,* and *risk tolerance.*

3. Balance the synergistic benefits of whatever form of diversification you are considering with the known and potential risks involved.

4. Start by "massaging" your current products or services. Alter pricing, modify or upgrade products you now market, etc. Visualize both the horizontal and vertical opportunities that expanding your existing offerings would create.

5. Initially move into untapped and less competitive niches within your current market parameters where and when your brand name is a plus.

6. When considering entering a new market, conduct your "due diligence" homework thoroughly. Assess your opportunity from the prospective buyer's vantage point. Check competition. Consider what actions these competitors may take should you move into "their territory."

7. Conduct a broad overview of any new potential market. Does such an analysis suggest long-term opportunities? Has any potential market already advanced technologically?

For example, has it been subjected (in manufacturing jargon) to the latest innovations, such as SCP (smart, connected products)? Note comment on "ripple effect" below.

8. Develop a practical, strategic plan that starts with the preparation and concludes with post-implementation actions. Include a budget addressing just this diversification venture. Keep separate figures. Edit the plan as it unfolds, making necessary adjustments along the way. Hold review sessions periodically.

9. Engage the support of your employees, particularly those that might be affected in *any* way by this program. Involve them early on. Reward them (with praise or financially) for their extra effort. Keep them updated on developments.

10. Consider when and how to launch your diversification program. The timing should allow for glitches, and the support should cover all advertising and sales promotional efforts.

11. Be prepared for the unexpected. Nothing goes exactly as planned. The most common problem issue is timing. New ventures seem to take longer than anticipated. They *always* do. Costs typically exceed budget.

Tip: Don't overlook the care and maintenance of your existing products. They are what got you where you are in the first place.

The Ripple Effect

To maximize your opportunity for a successful effort, it behooves you to position any proposed program on what I call "the ripple scale."

We are all familiar with what happens when a person tosses a rock into the middle of a still-water pond. The expanding waves are the most immediate and most powerful near the splash point. These waves decrease in size to ripples as they expand, diminishing over time and size in proportion to the distance from the initial impact point.

Fallout opportunities that extend from any splash point (yours or other outside sources') can be complex, diverse, and widely varying over time.

Tip: Ride the full body of these wave opportunities rather than be left behind in their wake.

Reference chapter 1 for comments on the tides of change.

Take the impact of technology, for example. It has become an increasingly all-encompassing force in recent years. A ripple-fallout sub-component is *artificial intelligence* (AI). The concept of AI has been around for some two hundred years—replacing labor with machinery. However, recently, under the subcategory referred to as "deep learning," its impact has become much more pervasive.

Modern "thinking" machines require more educated operators, which, in turn, increases the stratification of society by requiring that the workforce be better educated. This evolving societal shift has fostered all sorts of ripple effects, both rapid (the computer) and slow (education). Keep the magnitude of this shift in mind as you investigate diversification opportunities.

Another "ripple" example stems from the impact of e-commerce's rapid growth. This expansion has forced major carriers to, in turn, expand their facilities. FedEx's quarterly profits were squeezed last Christmas as the package delivery giant strained to keep up with the surge in holiday shopping, particularly online. *The Wall Street Journal* reports that FedEx has opened four new distribution hubs and nineteen automated sorting stations to accommodate the more than one million packages it now processes daily.

It is worth mentioning that total retail sales grew nationwide in 2017, but retail store revenues went down as e-commerce moved in. A measure of this change is that the number of store (brick and mortar) closings was the greatest since the recession year 2000. A further developing "ripple" may be the conversion of large box stores to such diverse uses as e-commerce delivery centers and exercise facilities, e.g., Planet Fitness gymnasiums with their fifteen hundred club locations.

Did you ride the crest of the Internet wave in your market area?

As a closing review, I suggest you analyze any diversification plans in terms of the following:

- *Consumer need.* Is there a valid and expanding market requirement for your diversification venture? The focus should be *on what the buyer seeks and will accept, not on what you would like to have happen.*

- *Opportunity.* Can the designated marketplace absorb another entry? Is the market growing, and if so, how fast and in what direction? What are your competitive advantages? How do you plan to secure a market foothold (through price or another method)? What are the risks, and what are the rewards?

- *Technological innovation.* Is the market segment you intend to pursue through diversification subject to rapid technological innovation (i.e., automation, artificial intelligence, biotechnology, nanotechnology, etc.)? If so, how might you utilize this technology, harnessing its power for your benefit?

- *Return on investment.* How long will it take you to recoup your monetary investment in this proposed venture? A reasonable target would be two years to break even and three years for a total return. I would be very cautious about accepting less than a three-year break-even projection with a five-year total return. In the latter case, the risk may be excessive. A good question to ask: how does your diversified projected rate of growth compare with your current ongoing rate of market penetration?

There are five classic categories for assessing any new offering: product, price, promotion, place, and *positioning.* They too can serve as a final checklist for your plans.

The next and most important step is *taking action.* Remember, careful preparation will mitigate your level of risk. List *all* synergistic benefits (revenue, distribution, net financial, accounting, morale, competition, customer reaction—to name just a few) before moving forward. Don't forget to manage those risks. Good hunting.

A final and current positive illustration. Amazon is, arguably, one of the leading growth companies in the world today. It continually reinvents itself, employing a mixed strategy of diversification and evolution. Since going public in 1997, it has launched several specialty enhancements, such as Prime service in February 2005. It then diversified by adding Amazon web services (a cloud computing arm) in March 2006; it then introduced Kindle in November 2007. Then it introduced its voice-response Echo speaker at approximately the same time.

A revised delivery service is next. Speaking of the laws of innovation!

Takeaway

Change is an ever-present factor in our lives. In this era, it appears to be moving at an accelerating rate. *Recognize change and harness its power, or risk being left behind.*

Reflections

In closing, do I, the author, suggest that a company pursue diversification or some facet thereof? My feeling is that involvement with diversification may become inevitable if a company is to continue to grow. For this reason, some form of growth through "branching out" should be considered as an important growth strategy to be further pursued when corporate timing is appropriate and opportune.

APPENDIX

Examples often provide the best illustrations of parameters and possibilities. Following are diversification developments, many of which may be familiar, as they have been extracted from timely business publications such as *The Wall Street Journal, The New York Times,* and *The Economist.*

Tweaks

- *Snack foods.* Purchased out of bankruptcy by an investment group in 2013, Hostess Brands, LLC, made several strategic adjustments to revitalize its key brand, Twinkies. Key to the brand's turnaround has been doubling the product's shelf-life (to reduce manufacturing costs and to extend its sell-by date) and creating a deep-fried version. These tweaks have been successful enough to allow the owners to plan for a corporate return to the public stock market.

New Products—Same Market

- *Beverages.* Coca-Cola has launched a new initiative, which it calls Beverages for Life. Rather than have one product that serves all our needs Coca-Cola is offering beverages targeted for all types of people at all stages of their lives and for a variety of purposes

New Markets—Same Product

- *Automotive.* Saudi Arabia's recent decision to allow women to drive is projected to boost the car market. Already BMW (Mini Cooper), Ford Motor Company, and Volkswagen have launched specific ads targeted toward the female market in that country.

- *Bottled coffee.* The Dunkin' Brands Group recently announced that in early 2016, it is introducing its coffee product in bottled form into the retail food market. The Dunkin' product is now being distributed by Coca-Cola in competition with Starbuck's Frappuccino, which is distributed by Pepsico. This could also be classified in the new product/new market category.

- *Canal.* The Panama Canal's decision (and investment) to expand its lock size (completed in June 2016) has already enhanced its United States- bound shipping tonnage. The result has been a revenue increase of tens of million dollars in toll revenue, notes the *Wall Street Journal*. In a sense, this represents acquisition of a new market previously serviced by transportation through the Suez Canal.

New Product—New Market (Reinventions)

- *Internet.* Google, the software communications giant, announced plans to introduce Pixel, a Smartphone of its own.

- *Consumer products.* Mars, Inc., the well-known candy manufacturer, is shifting the emphasis of its business from chocolates to the faster-growing pet food business. Mars already had a fledgling pet-care division, but with the acquisition of VCA, a veterinary and dog-care business, Mars now plans to generate the majority of its revenue from this faster-growing and more profitable field.

- *A true mix.* Elon Musk has generated one of the most creative and interesting diversification strategies. He fathered PayPal, Tesla Motors, Solar City, SpaceX, and recently, Neuralink (linking the human mind to artificial intelligence). All these enterprises are quite different. If there is a commonality, it is Elon's conceptual genius.

Vertical Diversification and Integration

- *Travel service.* TripAdvisor, a world leader in online reservations booking, has launched a direct booking service into the reservations market. TripAdvisor seeks a source of additional revenue, hoping that its traveler-audience will stay on their website and book directly.

  Thus far, results have been mixed. Revenues have declined for the first time in TripAdvisor's history. However, its corporate executives are optimistic that this form of diversification will eventually be productive. The TripAdvisor example might also be categorized as a new market entry.

- *Amazon.* Amazon (see chapter 9, "Vertical Integration") has announced plans to develop its own distribution capability to accelerate speed of delivery. Besides experimenting with a drone delivery vehicle, it opened twenty-three warehouses in the second half of 2016 (as opposed to three in the first half of that year). Such vertical distribution is noteworthy for two factors. First, Amazon's volume size (enormous). Second, the proposed (exploratory) introduction of delivery with drones directly to customers. Federal Express is now experimenting with drone delivery, and United Parcel Services are undoubtedly monitoring Amazon's activities closely.

- *Apple.* Recently introduced at the Worldwide Developers' Conference was Apple's HomePod, a voice-activated home speaker. The device is almost double ($349) the price of its Echo, which has sold approximately 11 million to-date. This is an example of an "upsell" strategy, in that most companies seek to reduce the value of their products rather than the other way around.

- **Tiffany.** The 180-year-old jeweler fired its chief executive when he introduced a three-year strategic plan that didn't forecast much profit improvement. Evidently, the plan continued the downward vertical attempt to sell lower-priced jewelry. Last year, 45 percent of Tiffany's sales came from jewelry categories with an average price under $530— degrading in both image and margin. Not all "down-sell" strategies are successful.

Please refer to my web page, brooksfenno.net, for author's notes and comments on more recent examples of diversification

INDEX

ACKNOWLEDGEMENTS

- Thomas Peterfly, Interactive Brokers
- Bill Stuart, W. P. Stuart and Co., Ltd.
- Eric DeLong, Acorn Manufacturing Co.
- Dan Rocconi, Bixby International Corporation
- Jill Kushner, Buyer Advertising
- Adam Chase, Chase Corporation
- Arthur McGinnes, MicroMedia of New England, Inc.
- Arthur Brussard, TruckCourier Inc.
- Jeff Whittemore, Zipwall
- Quinn Mills, Harvard Business School

Space below to list possible diversification options for your firm: